Advance Praise for
Write Your Own Story

"I'm so proud of my friend Patti Ann who has written a beautiful, honest, and emotional memoir. In the world of TV, you only see the 'perfect' version of ourselves, while behind the scenes life can get messy and complicated. If you're planning a career in broadcasting, Patti Ann gives you a wonderful road map on how to achieve your dreams. She also gives great advice on when might be the time to try something new. The bottom line is, it's always important to stay true to yourself, know what's precious in life, and the rest will fall into place."

—Janice Dean, Fox News Senior Meteorologist
and *New York Times* bestselling author

"Patti Ann Browne is the ultimate professional and a friend I have known for almost her entire career. Her memoir is a must-read: behind the scenes at cable news; her victories and crises; her strong, loving family; her son's courageous efforts to overcome serious health crises. All told with class and self-deprecating humor in a genuinely conversational tone. Patti Ann Browne is the real deal!"

—Peter King, Former US Congressman

"There is so much more to a TV news anchor's work than meets the viewer's eye—hours of preparation, rewrites, wardrobe, guests, laughter, mishaps. Patti Ann Browne's memoir of her career, and the life she has led off camera, is charming, funny, self-deprecating, and heart wrenching. Above all, as she now invites her viewers to see the 'big picture' of her life, she movingly reveals how she discovered the loving God as her real producer, who was always behind the scenes and present to every step she took."

—David G. Bonagura, Jr., Author of *Steadfast in Faith* and *Staying with the Catholic Church*

"Patti Ann has written a must-read memoir. From the Fordham University newsroom to Fox News Channel, she takes you on a journey of her personal and professional triumphs and disappointments. Along the way, life lessons are dispensed, making you feel like you have been friends for years."

—Carl Denaro, Author of *The Son of Sam and Me: The Truth About Why I Wasn't Shot by David Berkowitz*

Write Your Own Story

A MEMOIR

How I Took Control by Letting Go

Patti Ann Browne

Post Hill
PRESS

A POST HILL PRESS BOOK
ISBN: 978-1-63758-206-0
ISBN (eBook): 978-1-63758-207-7

Write Your Own Story:
How I Took Control by Letting Go
© 2022 by Patti Ann Browne
All Rights Reserved

Cover photo by Barry Morgenstein

This is a work of nonfiction. All people, locations, events, and situations are portrayed to the best of the author's memory.

Post Hill Press
New York • Nashville
posthillpress.com

Published in the United States of America
1 2 3 4 5 6 7 8 9 10

With gratitude to my parents,
who gave me the courage to pursue my dreams
and the faith to stay grounded throughout my life.

CONTENTS

AUTHOR'S NOTE

"Memory Lane is full of potholes."

-ANONYMOUS

This memoir is the true story of my life. Most of the events in this book took place years or even decades ago. I describe them as faithfully as my memory allows. But memories are not always reliable. I researched what I could, digging up old documents and photos. In cases where other people were involved, I tried to contact those people to ask if their accounts were consistent with mine. In some instances, tweaks were made as a result of those contacts. In all instances, I shared my story as honestly as I could.

There are things I chose to leave out. A memoir is like a photo album, but with words. When we choose pictures for an album, we pick the happy ones, the funny ones, the flattering ones. Likewise, my book is a selection of my favorite memories, although I tried to include some valleys along with the hills.

This memoir has some dramatic chapters and some much more lighthearted sections. If at any point you can't decide if I'm being serious or making a joke, it's safe to assume I was trying (and apparently failing) to be funny. Sometimes sarcastic humor doesn't come across well in print.

I wrote this book myself. There was no ghostwriter, and my editor took a "hands off" approach, correcting some punctuation and grammar but respecting my style and vision.

I hope you get something out of it. May God bless you as you write your own life story.

-PA

CHAPTER 1

Much Wanted, Strong-Willed

When the elevator doors opened onto the floor of the neonatal intensive care unit, it was obvious something was wrong. Mike and I, back from a brief lunch outside the hospital, were greeted by deafening sirens, flashing lights, and doctors and nurses running toward the room our son shared with several other premature babies. It was a code blue. My heart sank, and I said to my husband, "Something terrible is happening to someone's baby!"

We walked down the hall, trying to stay out of everyone's way, while I silently prayed for the poor family whose baby was in distress. We reached the large room and entered. I felt like I'd been punched in the gut.

"It's ours!" I wailed as we ran to Connor's incubator in the corner near the window.

We couldn't get too close. The top had been removed, and our tiny son was surrounded by doctors and nurses frantically trying to save his life. It wasn't going well. He was lifeless, dark purple, his monitor showing no signs of heartbeat or breathing. He looked so alone. A doctor was trying to insert a breathing tube into his impossibly small body. I heard the doctor mutter in a low but clearly frustrated voice, "I can't get a vent!"

"Connor!" I yelled, panic and despair quickly overtaking me. The doctors looked our way, and one said to a nurse, "Get them out of here."

She approached us and said, "I'm sorry, but you need to wait outside."

We were ushered out of the room, past the other babies' parents staring at us with fear and pity. The nurse noticed them and said, "All of you have to leave."

In the hall, barely able to speak, I asked her, "What happened? He was okay when we left!"

She said he had stopped breathing—something not uncommon in the NICU (fittingly pronounced "NICK-you" since it leaves scars on your heart). It had happened to Connor countless times in the 16 days since his birth at just 29 weeks. But in the past, the measures used to resuscitate him had worked. This time, they hadn't. He had crashed.

Standing in the hall, Mike and I desperately prayed. He called his parents while I called mine, imploring them to pray too. After what seemed like an eternity, a doctor came out. We looked at him hopefully. He shook his head and said, "Nothing yet."

I sank to the floor and cried, my back against the wall. Mike sat down next to me and held me.

How many minutes had passed? About five, Mike said.

And how many had passed before we got there? No way to know, he said.

If he's revived now, could he possibly be okay after so much time without oxygen?

My husband, a pediatrician who worked for that hospital and had done rotations in that NICU, assured me that some babies are fine even after a long time without oxygen. But I was looking in his eyes when he said it. There was fear in them.

And then he jumped up. "I have to go back in and baptize him."

It was a knife in my heart. That's when I knew we were probably going to lose him.

When Connor was born 11 weeks early, weighing barely two pounds, all four of our parents urged us to baptize him immediately. After all, he was in intensive care on breathing equipment. It was "touch and go." They even gave us special bottles of holy water to use for an emergency baptism. My parents brought us one from the Knock Shrine in our ancestral Irish home, County Mayo. Mike's parents gave us a bottle from Lourdes. Both bottles were at Connor's bedside, ready for use.

But Mike said no. Mike had seen many NICU babies during his practice, and he said Connor looked great for a preemie. His vitals were strong, and he was gradually gaining weight from my pumped breast milk, fed to him through the tiniest tube I'd ever seen. The other doctors agreed. Connor looked good.

There was no need for a hospital baptism. Our son would have a "real" christening in a church, surrounded by loved ones, followed by a big party. Under Catholic church rules, once a baby is baptized there can be no "do-over." So we should only baptize him in the NICU if he was about to die.

And there it was. Mike believed Connor was about to die. Maybe he was already gone. Left alone in the hall while Mike ran back into the room, I sobbed. The couples who'd been kicked out were standing nearby holding each other, many crying, too.

I called my parents back. My mom had clearly been crying. "Is he back?"

"No!" I answered hysterically. "Pray harder! Please! I can't lose him now! I can't!"

I prayed to God and bargained with Him. "God, please bring him back to me. I promise, I will raise him to love You. I love him. I need him back!"

I had waited so long for Connor. My career was my priority for too many years. I met Mike when I was 37, married him when I was 38, and had Connor when I was 39. I certainly wasn't the oldest woman ever to have a baby. But my obstetrician had made it clear that I was of "advanced maternal age." This put my baby at a higher risk for all sorts of bad things.

So I did everything right during my pregnancy—ate healthy; took prenatal vitamins; gave up caffeine, alcohol, artificial sweeteners. I read lots of books and followed all the advice.

But things started to go wrong early on. Just shy of three months, I was sitting in my office at Fox News Channel, preparing to solo anchor a live show. I stood up to head to the studio, and there was an enormous puddle of blood on my chair. Gripped by fear, I started rushing down the hall toward the bathroom, then realized I was dripping blood the whole way. I hurried back to my office.

I called my producer, Tom Lowell, and said, "I think I'm having a miscarriage!"

"You're pregnant?" he replied. I hadn't announced yet. "Stay where you are. I'm calling an ambulance!"

Distraught, I called Mike and my parents. Moments later, another producer, Dave Brown, knocked on my door. "What can I do?"

Dave tried to keep me calm while we waited for the EMTs. I tearfully told him I was sure I was losing the baby. I've known lots of women who've miscarried. I knew this was the sign.

When the EMTs arrived, they were sure too. I asked if there was any way this could be something else. One gently told me, "Given the amount of blood I'm seeing in your office and in the hall, it's unlikely."

They explained that there was nothing they could do to stop a miscarriage. They were taking me to the hospital just to keep me comfortable.

I cried as I was loaded onto a stretcher and wheeled down the hall. Colleagues stood at their cubicles, wishing me well. Word had spread fast. Chris Knowles, then a Fox meteorologist, yelled from his office door, "We're praying for you, Patti Ann." We turned a corner, and I saw my reflection in a full-length mirror in another anchor's office. My thick on-air mascara was running down my face with my tears. It was quite a sight. I couldn't care less. My heart was absolutely broken.

I remember thinking this was the worst day of my life. But miraculously, it was a false alarm. When we got to the hospital, a sonogram showed my baby, still there, with his little heart clearly beating, fast and strong. *Heart still beating.* Prayers answered. I rejoiced with Mike and my parents, who had met me at the ER.

But I now had a glimpse of the pain experienced by so many women—the devastation of losing a child through miscarriage. My heart aches for all of you who've been there.

I remember thinking we'll start again. I'll get pregnant again. But I already loved *this* baby. This baby was real. The love a pregnant woman has for her child is so strong. It's already a precious life.

After that scare, since doctors weren't sure what had caused the excessive bleeding, I was put on home bed rest. I stayed with my parents in Queens, since I needed to be "waited on" and Mike had to work. He visited often, and my sisters, Colleen and Mary Lou, would call. Fox VP John Moody checked in and told me to take all the time I needed. Fox was the most family-friendly shop I'd ever worked at. That's one of many reasons I stayed there for 17 years.

After six weeks of being pampered by my parents, I was cleared for regular activity again. There had been no more big bleeds, and sonograms showed the baby (who we now knew was a boy!) was growing.

I returned to work, and my Fox family expressed joy at hearing that my pregnancy was back on track. My longtime makeup artist, Iren Halperin, kindly reassured me with details of her own troubled pregnancy, which led to the birth of her healthy, beautiful daughter. As for the show I was about to anchor when I abruptly left, I was told someone grabbed the talented Laurie Dhue as she was walking out and threw her on set to sub for me, completely unprepared. She didn't miss a beat. Entertainment correspondent Bill McCuddy, the office comedian, joked that a "hazmat crew" had come in and cleaned up our office. (At least, I think he was joking.) Several colleagues mentioned that during my absence, my sometime co-anchor Julian Phillips had held regular prayer circles for my baby and for me. Fellow anchor Lauren Green also told me she had been praying, as did Geraldo Rivera, whose wife, Erica, was pregnant at the same time. I was truly blessed to have such wonderful co-workers. All seemed well.

But it wasn't.

At 24 weeks and six days (a pregnancy is supposed to be 40 weeks), I was vacuuming our living room in advance of a visit from Mike's parents to our apartment in Manhattan. I felt a big gush.

Assuming it was another bleed, I dropped the vacuum and rushed to the bathroom. Mike saw me and followed.

I was relieved to tell him it was just some clear fluid pouring out of me, not blood.

He looked in the toilet and his face went pale.

"It's amniotic fluid," he said in a low voice. "Your water just broke."

"What?" I scoffed, almost laughing. "No, my water did not break. I'm only at 24 weeks! What else could it be?"

"It's amniotic fluid. We have to get you to the hospital. What do you need me to pack?"

"We can't go the hospital," I replied, still in remarkable denial. "Your parents are coming for dinner."

Mike, who is both a doctor and a pragmatist, again insisted, speaking slowly now. "Your water just broke. What do you need me to pack for the hospital?"

Finally starting to comprehend the gravity of the situation, I said, "I don't know! I haven't gotten to that part of the books yet. I'm only at 24 weeks!"

He threw some stuff in a bag, and we caught a cab to the hospital.

On the way, he called my Uncle Rob and Aunt Helen, who also lived in Manhattan, and asked them to take our dog, Hunter, from our apartment. As I sat trembling uncontrollably in the taxi, I heard him ask them to be prepared to keep the dog for a while.

Once at the hospital, Mike told the reception desk that my water broke. Hearing how early I was, a doctor "explained" that it was probably just urine. It's common for pregnant women to "leak" a little, due to increased pressure on their bladder.

Mike and I both insisted that it was definitely not urine. We also told them about my earlier problems. But unfortunately, we had not retrieved a sample of the fluid from the toilet. (Please do this if you end up in a similar situation.) So the doctor was unconvinced, and instructed me to walk laps around the floor while wearing a pad, in hopes that I would leak again so they could test the fluid.

In retrospect, this was astonishingly irresponsible advice. After several laps, I did leak again, and they analyzed the material on the pad. Discovering that it was, in fact, amniotic fluid, they put me on a bed and told me to move as little as possible.

A different doctor came into our room and ominously led with "I'm sorry." She confirmed that my amniotic sac had ruptured, and my pregnancy had taken a dramatic turn for the worse. She said premature rupture typically leads to labor within 24 to 48 hours.

If that were to happen, she calmly rattled off a long and devastating list of complications our son was likely to suffer for his entire life. Premature babies are at risk for breathing problems, muscle weakness, heart abnormalities, intestinal issues, hearing and vision problems, neurological disorders, poor immunity, and social difficulties.

That list is for babies born at 37 weeks or less. I was less than 25 weeks along. There have been babies born even earlier who have done well, but the doctor warned that statistically speaking, the prognosis was not good. Babies born at this stage often didn't even survive. And those who did struggled. She said while advances had been made in caring for premature babies, there was a limit to what doctors could do.

Contemplating my son's future with severe health problems, I cried so hard my whole body was heaving and shuddering. I asked the doctor if there was anything I could do to postpone his birth. Without a trace of irony, she said it was essential that I stay positive and think happy thoughts. Oh, and try not to move or shake.

She said that in some cases, a ruptured membrane does not lead to imminent labor. While an early rupture usually means the body is trying to push the baby out due to infection or some other complication, sometimes the sac ruptures for no apparent reason, and it doesn't induce labor.

In those cases, the mother can sometimes stave off delivery for a week or two, despite the womb being compromised. I was not in labor—no contractions, no dilating. And there were no signs of infection or fetal distress. The doctors were already remarking that the baby's vitals were excellent given the situation. He was a fighter. So I could possibly buy my son more time in the womb by staying hospitalized on strict bed rest. The average, for babies not delivered within that first one to two days, is 10 days. Some women go longer. The doctor explained that every day he stayed inside me would make a huge difference.

So I was wheeled to a room in the maternity ward, where I was told to stay flat on my back to eliminate downward pressure on my womb. Since my sac was ruptured, our son was swimming in low fluid. I was being given intravenous liquids to replenish the fluid in the sac, but every time it reached a certain level, it would leak out onto my pad. The sac's fluid level was periodically measured by sonogram. It was usually between 10 and 30 percent of what it should be. Not comfortable for the baby.

I was not allowed to sit up, other than briefly for meals. I wasn't supposed to stand or walk to the bathroom (a bed pan was nearby).

I was given steroid shots to speed up the baby's lung development, and antibiotics to ward off infection. Every so often, a contraption on my mattress would inflate around my legs, squeezing them to get the blood flowing and avoid clots, since I was dangerously immobile. A fetal monitor was strapped across my stomach, as well as a separate monitor for my own heart. My temperature was taken frequently. If either of us showed signs of infection or distress, the baby would have to come out.

I was determined that this would not happen. I wanted this baby more than anything. I resolved to stay calm and happy, lying on my back staring at the ceiling, marinating in my own sweat, for as long as possible. I prayed to God to keep my son comfortable in his low-water environment. I prayed that both of us would avoid infection, despite the fact that my womb was now exposed. I looked around at my new home. There was pretty flowered wallpaper trim just under the ceiling (I can still picture it perfectly). A TV was mounted very high up on the wall. I could do this. One day at a time.

I was there for 31 days.

The morning after my first night there, Mike came to my room and suggested we decide on a name. Of course, we had started talking about it earlier. But we had only gotten as far as tossing around ideas, thinking we had many more months to choose one. Now it seemed we would only have days or hours.

We agreed we liked Irish names, although both of us are also part German, and Mike has other ethnicities mixed in as well.

I said, "Throw out a name you like."

He said, "Connor."

I loved it. I said, "When you go home tonight, please look it up and find out what it means."

The next morning, Mike showed up in my room grinning, waving a computer printout.

"Connor," he said, "means much-wanted and strong-willed."

It was perfect.

"Also," he continued, "lover of hounds."

Our dog, Hunter, was a hound.

I smiled. "Well, I guess we have our name."

Since Mike worked at the hospital, he was able to stop by my room often. On days when the baby's vitals started to look iffy, he slept in a chair next to my bed. My parents and sisters also visited, as well as Mike's parents and sister. Other friends and family offered to come, but I usually declined. They reasonably assumed I must be going out of my mind with boredom. But oddly, that wasn't the case. There were some bad days, but overall, I was at peace. And I was wary of too much excitement.

I knew my job was to lie in this bed and relax, and it was an incredibly important job. My sister Colleen printed out large photos of my family and Hunter, and taped them high up on the walls to keep me company and make me feel more at home.

Every morning, my nurse would enter the room smiling and say, "I can't believe you're still here!" There was a calendar on the wall, and every day I felt gratitude when the nurse put an "X" through another number.

I spent some of my time educating myself on the care of a premature baby. Mike bought me *The Premature Baby Book* by Dr. Sears. I found a way to prop it up on my food tray and read it while lying down. I was saddened to read that some mothers have difficulty bonding with their preemies. Premature infants aren't fat and soft and cuddly like full-term babies. They're bony, scrawny, and their skin is rough. Some moms have trouble adjusting. I stared at the photos of preemies, so that when I first laid eyes on my own, I would be prepared and happy.

Alisyn Camerota, then a Fox anchor, kindly called to offer me advice and encouragement. She had recently given birth to very premature twins. Her babies were doing great after a rough start in life. Her most important tip was to request a breast pump immediately after my son was delivered. When a baby is born months early, the mother's milk usually hasn't "come in" yet. It needs to be aggressively coaxed out—the sooner the better. Otherwise, it dries up, and there is no way to get that opportunity back. Even if Connor was too weak to nurse at first, he could still get my breast milk through a feeding tube. I filed this away in my mind.

I also prayed a lot and watched a ton of TV. One day, Mike was coming down the hall to see me and heard what he thought was loud crying from my room. He rushed in to find me laughing with Colleen, watching the movie *The Naked Gun* on the television. It's a crude, ridiculous movie, but my twin, also known as my "mind reader," had figured out I needed levity. After that, Mike showed up with a stack of DVDs of over-the-top comedies. Even during the most serious of times, it's important to laugh.

After a while, I was permitted to use the bathroom and even shower every few days. My Fox hair stylist, Carol Kandhai, called to say hi and ask what she could do. I described the situation to her, and she graciously came to cut my hair, which was long and caked with sweat. What a relief to have it off my neck.

Twenty-nine weeks and two days into my pregnancy, I lost a lot of fluid. Normally, Connor's vitals remained satisfactory even after a gusher. Not this time. I guess he had just had enough. His numbers started to fluctuate. They stabilized, but I was moved to the labor and delivery ward for the night, just in case.

In the middle of that night, I awoke concerned. I don't know why, other than that God was whispering to me. I glanced at the monitor. Connor's heart rate was not showing up. Not a big deal. Very often while I slept, the fetal monitor would shift off the baby, and I'd lose the heartbeat. After 31 days in the hospital, I knew how to slide the monitor around on my stomach until I found the beat again.

But this time no matter where I rolled that monitor, I could not find a heartbeat. I called to Mike, who was sleeping on the chair. He slid the monitor all around, then uttered a quiet expletive. He hurried out of the room.

Moments later, a team of doctors rushed in with a sonogram machine, Mike in tow. Within seconds, they had the device on my stomach, and I could see Connor's tiny form on the screen. What I could not see was a heartbeat. There was a faint blip, every so often. Way too weak and sluggish.

Another expletive from my husband.

The doctors urgently wheeled me out of the room on my bed, saying, "Your baby is going to be delivered right now by C-section."

As we hurtled down the hall, an anesthesiologist fired off questions about allergies and reactions, which I struggled to answer in my distress.

At the same time, Mike asked the surgeon, whom he knew from his residency, if he could be in the room.

The doctor replied, "Normally no, but since you're an attending physician, yes. Go scrub in!"

Mike was gone, and I was in the brightly-lit operating room, feeling like I had failed my son. It was too soon. I was still 11 weeks early. Connor had been "measured" earlier that day. It's not exact, but they use ultrasound to estimate weight. They had pegged him at less than two pounds. The doctors had told us outcomes were much better for babies born over two pounds. He was too small. He was too young.

A doctor commented that Connor's heartbeat was looking a little stronger.

I said, "Maybe this means we can wait. Give him more time?"

The surgeon replied, "Maybe, but it's probably just your adrenaline giving him a temporary boost. We need to prep you just in case."

I was lifted off my bed and onto the operating table.

I heard hushed gasps and muttering.

I turned my head.

The bed I had been removed from was drenched in blood.

"Mom's hemorrhaging!" the surgeon announced. "Now we *have* to operate or we might lose the mom. Get her blood typed and crossed, and have blood ready to transfuse."

So now they were concerned for both of our lives. This was it. It was happening now. And I might die. Connor might live without his mother—if he lived at all. Could Mike bear to lose both of us? And if he lived, Connor might be severely disabled. Could Mike handle that without me? I prayed. I begged for Connor's life and mine.

They drew a curtain across my waist.

Mike appeared at my side in scrubs. I told him, "I love you."

He said, "I love you too."

I was afraid those might be our last words. Mike looked worried. I didn't know it then, but he had seen the blood-soaked bed and was fully aware of the implications of that. He held my hand. The anesthesia was working, and I couldn't feel anything below my chest. I told the anesthesiologist I felt like I wasn't breathing. Maybe

I was dying. He said most patients feel that way during a C-section, but if I can talk, I can breathe. He said my vitals looked fine. I tried to stay calm.

I was awake through it all, and after mere minutes, a voice from the other side of the curtain said, "He's out! Good tone!"

He was alive. Our miracle baby! I heard no crying, but I knew from the preemie book that most premature infants are too weak to cry.

I turned to Mike, still holding my hand. "He's out?" I asked. "How does he look?"

Mike peeked around the curtain and looked pleased.

"He looks great! Big!"

I yelled, "Hi Connor! I'm your mommy! I love you!"

Then they whisked him out of the room. I still hadn't seen him. The doctors said they were sewing me up.

"So am I okay?" I asked. "What about the bleeding?"

They were already past that. "Oh, you're fine. Whatever that was, it wasn't life-threatening."

I turned to Mike. "Go stay with Connor."

He left, looking like a proud daddy. I said a prayer of thanks.

We had it all planned in advance. The preemie book said if you already know you're having a preemie, have a plan in place. You're going to want someone to stay with the baby. That would be Mike. But that leaves the mom alone, so plan to call someone when the delivery is starting, so they can come and stay with the mom. Mike had called my mother, who had called my sister Colleen, who lives in another state. It was midnight. They both came. We had all been waiting a long time for this moment. And so far, things looked good. I was happy.

As I recovered, I asked them how their drives to the hospital had gone. My mom replied that she got terribly lost and finally asked a cop, "How do you get to Broadway?"

I joked, "And the cop replied: 'Practice, practice, practice.'" Colleen was pleasantly surprised that I was telling goofy jokes when my son had just been born 11 weeks premature. It showed how truly elated I was by the news that Connor seemed healthy. (I was also high on some sort of pain-killing drug cocktail the hospital had put in my IV.)

While my mom stayed by my side, Colleen went to find Mike and Connor. She returned, saying she was allowed to take me to them. I was moved to a wheelchair, which she steered through the halls. As we approached the NICU nursery, I could hear a baby crying incredibly loudly. My motherly instinct kicked in.

I said, "That's my Connor crying!"

"No," Colleen replied gently. "Remember, you read that preemies don't cry because their lungs are underdeveloped? Connor isn't crying."

She later told me it was the detail that had pained her the most when she saw him earlier. She was prepared for him to be tiny, but not for the silence. He was so quiet. It was unnatural and heartbreaking.

We entered the room and there was Mike, holding the tiniest, loudest baby I'd ever seen. Connor was beet red and crying at the top of his little lungs. It was music to my ears.

"He's crying!" I said proudly to Mike.

"He sure is!"

Colleen was overjoyed to see that Connor had already gained enough strength to cry.

"He looks like an alien!" I observed, beaming with love.

Mike and Colleen both laughed. Well, it was true. He looked like a frog with ET's head—even smaller than most of the pictures in the book. But he was beautiful to me.

I wasn't allowed to hold him yet (Mike could, because he was a doctor in scrubs), but I talked to him and let him wrap his tiny finger around mine. It seemed to calm his crying. Then he had to go to his new home, his Isolette incubator.

I went back to my room with my mom and requested a breast pump.

Connor weighed two pounds, six ounces at birth. That's very small, but since we were expecting a baby under two pounds, we were thrilled. His Apgar scores (which assess an infant's overall health at birth) were good, and his vital stats were decent, considering the circumstances.

But his lungs were underdeveloped, and he was on breathing equipment known as CPAP (continuous positive airway pressure). And it seemed like every inch of his tiny body had something taped to it and wires coming out of it. His monitor beeped frequently, alerting us to bradycardias (heart slowdowns requiring intervention), apnea (slowed breathing), and "de-sats" (decreased oxygen saturation).

He was jaundiced, so he had to lie blindfolded under special lights for six days, which is not uncommon, but it just increased his apparent discomfort. A brutal spinal tap when he ran a fever added insult to injury. I spent most of every day at Connor's side. Mike and I were allowed to hold him for brief periods at first, then longer periods as he got stronger.

Studies show that preemies benefit medically and emotionally from skin-to-skin contact with their parents (known as kangaroo care). So I would rest him against my chest, my elbows propped up on a Boppy pillow, his wires still attached to the monitor, a robe wrapped around us both. I sang to him and read him lots of stories. Relatives would visit, welcoming him to the family, speaking at first into the holes of his incubator, letting him grab their fingers, later holding him when allowed. He seemed pretty content.

The nurses taught me how to "stimulate" him to get his heart back up to speed when his alarm went off. Sometimes loudly yelling his name was enough. Other times he needed his foot tickled or squeezed, or his back tapped. As the days went by, his monitor was beeping less, and he required less stimulation to be revived.

Things were moving in the right direction.

Until they weren't.

After about two weeks, things started going backwards. He started de-saturating more frequently, and it was taking longer to revive him. I mentioned it to the doctors during morning rounds (the only time I saw them all day). They were not concerned. They said there's often a "honeymoon phase" after which a preemie might have a few setbacks, but it's nothing to worry about.

But it got alarmingly worse. The de-sats were downright scary. He wasn't responding to simple stimulation. The nurses had to resort to more dramatic interventions. A few times, he turned gray. One time he went past gray to blue, and for the first time required "bagging" (an inflating bag to push oxygen into a mask placed over his face).

As his mom, who had kept vigil over him for weeks, I could tell Connor was different. His body looked tense and his facial expression, which had been pretty relaxed, was now a constant wince.

The doctors suspected infection and put him on antibiotics, but he continued to go downhill.

Finally, during morning rounds on day 16, a NICU nurse recommended that the doctors give him a blood transfusion. They were dismissive at first, but she was persistent. She told them he was "quite symptomatic" and mentioned having to bag him. They agreed, and a transfusion was begun a few hours later.

Exhausted from all the worry, having barely left Connor's side for days as his condition deteriorated, I now felt comfortable getting a quick lunch with Mike across the street. The doctor said it would take a few hours for the transfusion to improve Connor's condition, but I was relieved knowing the "cure" was at last underway. Plus, I was starving.

So we left Connor in his incubator, confident that life-saving blood was now coursing through his veins. We returned from lunch to find our infant son coding. He wasn't breathing, and there were no signs of life. After we were escorted from the room, precious minutes passed as we waited in the hall, aware that each passing second meant a potentially worse future for Connor, if he survived at all.

As the doctors struggled to save Connor, Mike re-entered the room and grabbed one of the bottles of holy water from the nightstand next to his incubator.

"Excuse me," he said, trying to clear a path between two nurses to stand beside Connor's unresponsive body. One of the nurses later told us she thought Mike had gone mad and was hoping to save Connor himself. But the other nurse saw it.

"He's baptizing him! Let him through."

Mike quickly prayed, "I baptize you in the name of the Father, Son, and Holy Spirit."

He used the holy water to make a sign of the cross on Connor's cold, gray forehead. Mike has never told anyone which bottle he used. Not even me.

As quickly as he ran in, Mike left so the doctors could continue their work. Waiting in the hall, I scanned Mike's face for a sign of hope. There was none.

"Still nothing," he said.

"It's been too long," I exclaimed. "Too long!"

But soon a doctor emerged, looking somber but more upbeat than earlier.

Removing his mask, he said, "He's back."

I almost couldn't believe my ears.

"Thank God!" we both exclaimed.

But we were almost afraid to ask the follow-up.

"How is he?"

The doctor replied, "It's too soon to say. Anything can happen. He's intubated, but so far he looks good. Sometimes when babies emerge from an episode like this, their eyes aren't focused, their color is off, and they appear dazed. That's an indication the oxygen loss may have caused brain damage. But once we got an airway into your son, his color instantly went back to pink, and he started tugging at the breathing tube, which is a great sign. It's like he was saying, 'What the hell is this thing down my throat? Get it out of me!' We literally had to fight with him to stop him from yanking out the vent. He's a tough cookie. I'm cautiously optimistic."

A wave of relief came over me. "Can we see him?"

"Sure. You can't touch him. But you can see him."

We hurried to Connor's Isolette, and there he was—pink again, breathing again, looking at us through the glass when we called his name. He looked exhausted, not surprisingly, and the ventilator looked horribly uncomfortable, but he was back. It seemed miraculous that this was the same baby who 10 minutes earlier had showed no signs of life and was ash-colored from lack of oxygen.

I told him I loved him, my arms draped over the top of the incubator, my face pressed against the glass, tears streaming down my cheeks.

Much wanted. Strong willed. Connor.

CHAPTER 2

Triangles and Squares

My own birth story also had some drama. My mom didn't even know she was carrying me until I was born. Okay, that's completely true but highly misleading! My mom had no idea she was having *twins*. My mom was enormous when she was pregnant, but doctors were convinced she was having one huge baby. Sonograms were not routine when I was born back in the Dark Ages. And due to the way my sister and I were positioned in the womb, only one heartbeat could be heard with the stethoscope.

So doctors were standing by with a catcher's mitt, expecting to deliver Baby Godzilla, and instead Colleen squeaked out—weighing less than five pounds. At that point, the obstetrician said something like, "Hmm, there might be someone else in there."

Four minutes later, I was born. Surprise!

Actually, my mom says a nurse examined her a few hours before delivery and told her she was having twins. But my mom replied that the doctor had said it was one big baby. Unconvinced, the nurse touched my mom's stomach and said, "Nope. Feel here…one leg… another leg…another leg. At least three legs… Two babies. Twins!"

When the doctor returned, my mom mentioned what the nurse had said, and the doctor said, "She's a nurse. I'm the doctor. One baby."

Great, so now my mom was worried she was about to have a three-legged baby. Luckily for all of us, the doctor was wrong.

Colleen and I were both healthy, although small, as is typical with twins. But since my parents had had no idea they were bringing *two* babies home from the hospital, they only had one of everything. Colleen got the crib (you know, firstborn and all), so I spent my first few nights sleeping in a drawer. (Connor heard this story years later and asked, "Did they at least keep the drawer open?" Yes, Connor, yes.)

My parents married young and here they were, less than a year later, with two infants in a one-bedroom apartment in Queens. And less than a year after that, my sister Mary Lou was born. That made us "Irish triplets," as the expression goes. My two sisters are my best friends.

My mom stayed home with the three babies while my dad commuted to his entry-level job in the city. My dad's parents stopped by a lot with food. "Oh, there was a big sale on tenderloin, so we got an extra."

My paternal grandparents had immigrated to America from Ireland, separately, when they were teens. They knew what it was like to struggle. When Colleen and I visited Ireland after college, we saw the tiny house our grandfather Browne grew up in. It was eye-opening. He had been one of nine children living in a rustic, three-room dwelling on some low-lying farmland in County Mayo without modern utilities. But it sure was beautiful.

After arriving in New York, my grandfather worked for a meat-packing company, did some landscaping in the Hamptons, and had a delivery route for Thomas' English Muffins. He did whatever he could as an Irishman right off the boat who had never finished elementary school and faced discrimination. My grandmother stayed home to raise my dad, his sister, and his brother.

After two decades in America, my grandparents had saved enough to send all three of their kids to college. They were not wealthy, but they considered themselves very fortunate. What they had, they shared with us, as well as sending care packages back "home" to relatives on the Emerald Isle.

My grandfather never forgot his humble upbringing. He passed on his strong work ethic and belief in the American dream to my dad and his siblings.

Meanwhile, my mom's mother helped out tirelessly as my mom struggled to care for three infants. My mom says she never could've gotten through those first few years without our grandmother. After being up all night feeding and changing the three of us, my mom would catch a nap during the day while my grandmother took over. But Grammy had trouble telling Colleen and me apart. Once, my mom woke up to find one of us vomiting from having over-eaten, and the other crying from being hungry. Mary Lou was fine, but apparently Grammy had fed one of the twins twice. In her defense, we looked really alike! Even I can't tell who's who in baby pictures.

My mom's family wasn't well off, either. My mom grew up in a small attached house in Queens with her mother, father, and three siblings. Her father was a boilermaker who battled alcoholism and died when he was 53. My mom and her older sister Maureen were married by then, but my grandmother, a 50-year-old woman who had only been a homemaker, had to find a job to pay the bills. So, she worked as a secretary for decades, which suited her since she liked to stay busy.

If you dropped in on Grammy unexpectedly, you might find her cooking a big meal, or up on a ladder putting up crown molding. No matter what she was doing, she always wore a skirt and blouse. Always. Finally, when she was in her 70s, my mom gave her a velour pantsuit for her birthday, thinking her mother might want to be comfortable for a change when she was doing housework. (Believe it or not, velour pantsuits were in style at the time, thanks to *The Golden Girls*.) I can still picture the funny face Grammy made as she held up the garment to survey it.

"What am I supposed to do with this?"

"It's for wearing around the house," my mom said. "It's a lounge suit."

My grandmother tossed it back in the box and scoffed, "As if I lounge!"

Oh well, you can't blame my mom for trying.

Grammy lived to age 93, and in all those years I'm pretty sure she never lounged.

So both of my parents knew the value of a dollar and the rewards of hard work. They scrimped and saved, and when I was five we moved out of the apartment and into a house. We loved that house! It was warm and inviting, despite the fact that it was on a somewhat busy street in Queens and lacked a few modern conveniences such as air conditioning. On hot nights, the window fan didn't help much, and I would periodically soak my head in the sink and then go back to my pillow with dripping wet hair to stay cool. And there was one shower/bath for the five of us. Getting ready to leave the house in the morning required patience and speed.

We certainly weren't poor, but my parents' motto was to always live below your means. My mom would buy fabric and a pattern from the sewing supplies store and make matching dresses for the three of us. She also made her own clothes. We would keep the same car for 15 years or more. We didn't update our kitchen every 10 years like some of our neighbors. We had a black and white TV long after most of our friends had color. We went to the movies maybe once a year, and we certainly didn't waste our money on the overpriced popcorn. And we didn't spend our free time at the mall.

I thought maybe we weren't as well off as some of our friends. But I discovered later that my parents were saving for a rainy day and for the future. They also understood that the best things in life are free.

We went to the park or beach in the summer and spent time with our friends, the Walshes, at their shore house in Black Point, Connecticut. We belonged to a community pool where I became a decent swimmer. My dad's best friend, Barry Heine, had a boat, and we spent many summer weekends riding around Long Island's bays and harbors. My sisters and I learned how to fish at a young age and were waterskiing when we were 11. We also took a week's vacation every year at a modest resort in the Hamptons with a fun group of friends.

In the winter, we went sleigh-riding down a steep local hill when it snowed. Every night, we had family dinner—the five of us sitting around the table discussing our day. Our parents lent an understanding ear to all our problems and gave great advice. We celebrated the holidays with enthusiasm, decorating for all the seasons. Every winter, we picked out a Christmas tree from the local lot and, after loading it with ornaments, my dad would declare, "Best tree ever!"

Reflecting on my younger years, I realize that our most intense memories are not necessarily of events, but rather of feelings— especially the emotions of our parents. My very earliest memories are of times when my mother got extremely emotional.

One memory is of sitting in the lobby of a hospital with my two sisters and my dad. It was 1968 and I was three years old. My mom had left us to go somewhere inside the hospital. She later returned and burst into tears. Horrible, heart-wrenching sobs. It was the sound of incomprehensible sadness. My sisters and I felt helpless and scared. It was the first time we had seen our mother cry.

My dad said something about Vietnam and how we were lucky to still have Uncle Tom, because the person next to him in the vehicle had died. But my mom's younger brother was in bad shape. I later learned he had been sitting in the back of a truck coming back from a patrol when it hit a mine. He was choppered to a hospital in Vietnam, where he told doctors he couldn't move his neck. They wrapped a belt around his chin and told him not to move. X-rays revealed a fracture to his C-2 vertebra. A few days later, they drilled holes in his head and inserted bolts with wire to hold it still. They also operated on his shattered leg and foot.

Uncle Tom was airlifted to an army hospital in Japan, where he was immobilized in a full-body brace called a Stryker frame. Back home, my mom and the rest of her family got the devastating telegrams and everyone was praying like crazy. My mom's neighbor, Joan Lucey, contacted her uncle who happened to be an American priest doing missionary work in Yokohama. Fr. Newell visited Uncle Tom in the hospital and helped him make phone calls to his young wife Jean and my grandmother. Uncle Tom says Fr. Newell's help in this crisis was "a wonderful gift."

Aunt Jean quickly got herself a passport and flew to Uncle Tom's side in Japan with Fr. Newell's assistance. Jean later flew home with Tom on a brutal 18-hour flight on an army hospital plane with other severely wounded soldiers.

Thank God, my uncle recovered after a difficult nine-month stay at St. Albans Naval Hospital in Queens. My great-grandfather, Charles, took two buses every week to visit his grandson and everyone else on Tom's floor. They all called my grandmother's dad "Grandpa." My Great-Grandpa was a warm and charismatic man. I had the privilege of getting to know him before he died when I was 17, six years after his wife, Great-Grandma Anna, died.

Uncle Tom received a Purple Heart medal. He and Aunt Jean are now happily retired in Florida. They have two beautiful daughters and a grandson. But Uncle Tom's scars—physical and emotional— remain. And I will never forget my mother's pain. War is hell.

My other very early memory is much happier, although I didn't understand it at the time. It is of the moon landing in 1969. My mom excitedly sat my sisters and me on the rug in front of the tiny TV in our apartment. I now know that we were watching the splashdown after the astronauts returned to earth. At the time, all I knew was that my mom was losing her bleeping mind. She kept exclaiming that we were watching history in the making! This seemed odd, since all we saw was water.

But Mom was visibly nervous and told us to pay close attention! So we did, and eventually a "triangle" appeared in the water, and my mom was wildly ecstatic. I remember what was going through my three-year-old head as I stared at the screen: "A triangle in the water! A triangle in the water! Very important! Mom's going crazy! Pay attention! A triangle in the water!"

I didn't comprehend that three astronauts, just back from the moon, were in that triangular capsule. But to this day, I vividly recall sitting on that rug, staring at that black and white image of a triangle in the water, while my mom flipped out about how amazing this was. She was right, and I'm glad I witnessed it.

When I was a few years older, my mom again displayed strong emotion about something I did not yet understand. My sisters and I had a friend our age, whom I'll call Marie. She was funny, and all three of us enjoyed her company. We spent a lot of time with her.

But we did notice that she often showed up at our house unannounced—sometimes at inconvenient times. Yet my mom always seemed happy to see her. She'd say, "Hello, Marie! We're just sitting down to dinner. Why don't you join us?"

One day, my sisters and I, all around 10 years old, were in the kitchen, and I said to my mom, "Mom, you always tell us it's rude to visit someone without calling first, especially for dinner. But Marie shows up all the time, and you never tell her she should call first."

Mom spun around from the sink with eyes blazing and yelled, "Marie is welcome in this house ANY TIME, day or night!! She doesn't have to call; she doesn't need an invitation. She will ALWAYS BE WELCOME HERE!"

Now she looked like she was crying. My sisters and I quietly exchanged confused glances that said, *What's up with Mom?*

But none of us pursued it. This topic was clearly off-limits.

Many years later, my mom started to divulge more details about her childhood with an alcoholic father. She said she and her siblings would've been much better off if their mother had left him, but Grammy believed it was against her Catholic faith. (Actually, Catholics are allowed and encouraged to leave abusive relationships, even marital ones.) I asked my mom how she managed to stay so sane through all that.

She said prayer helped a lot. But she also had a neighbor, Joan Lucey, who lived around the corner. Whenever things got crazy, my mom left the house and ran around the corner to the Luceys' home. Joan's mom always welcomed her in and never asked questions. My mom says that to this day, she thanks God for the Luceys. She and Joan are still close. Joan and her sister were at my parents' 50th anniversary party a few years ago. They are wonderful people.

When my mom told me that story about the Luceys years ago, I remembered Marie. I said, "So that's why we always welcomed Marie to our house."

She said yes. She recognized the signs. In Marie, she saw herself as a child. She urged me to always be kind and to not ask too many questions if someone reached out for friendship or anything else. You just have no idea what other people are dealing with.

Always be a sanctuary for others, she said. It can literally change the course of someone's life.

I'm Facebook friends with Marie now, and I'm glad to say she is happily married to a terrific guy and has a beautiful family. I believe my mother might have actually played a small role in her happiness.

I was blessed to have a happy childhood. My dad kept advancing at his company—the corporate offices for a major department store. This enabled my sisters and me to attend the nearby Catholic elementary school. I ran track and did well in my studies. I sang in the church folk group and played the fife in the school's marching band. I won the Bishop Mugavero CYO Outstanding Youth Award for my various activities.

But I was not popular. If you looked up "square" in the dictionary back then, I think my photo was featured. I dressed like a tomboy, I didn't wear makeup, and I had no idea how to control my unruly auburn hair. I was a "teacher's pet," always raising my hand and correcting other kids' mistakes. At the pool during the summers, I would sit in a chair next to my mom and read while my sisters splashed around in the water with the other kids.

I didn't know how to get along with other people, so I usually just clung to Colleen, who was much more outgoing. Eventually, her friends would accept my presence. But I was definitely made fun of by some classmates, and I had a habit of turning tomato red when embarrassed. In fact, in our grammar school graduation yearbook, I was voted "Blushingest."

One of my most mortifying moments came on a day I had been looking forward to for most of my young life: my Communion Day. It's a very big day for Catholics, and I had been preparing for a year. The day finally arrived, and I received the Holy Eucharist for the first time. I felt like a princess walking down the aisle in my beautiful white lace dress and veil. The ceremony was lovely.

Afterwards, there was a big party for Colleen and me. It was a beautiful spring day, and our yard was filled with friends and family. I was in the driveway chatting with a neighbor and my dad when a wasp came along. The neighbor swatted it. As a general rule, it's not a great idea to anger a wasp. So now the wasp landed on my neck and stung me. I screamed and squirmed wildly, and the wasp fell down the back of my white dress, where I could feel it angrily buzzing around on my back. Of course, my screaming and thrashing drew the attention of all our guests.

My dad, standing next to me the whole time, knew that wasp was still in my dress, causing me severe distress. So he did what dads do: whatever he had to, to protect me from my attacker. Unfortunately, in this case, that involved ripping the back of my Communion dress open to get the wasp out, in front of all of our guests. There I stood, crying in the driveway in my undershirt and tights, my beautiful lace dress torn in half around my ankles, my neck throbbing in pain from the wasp sting, while my friends and family looked on awkwardly. I find this story hilarious now, but at the time, not so much.

My mom ran over and quietly scolded my dad. "You didn't have to do that."

"The wasp was in her dress, stinging her!" he responded.

My parents never argue in public. It's one of the reasons they've been happily married for more than 57 years. So hearing this brief exchange only increased my anguish. My dad was trying to protect me from physical harm, while my mom was trying to protect my pride.

I changed clothes; my mom treated and bandaged my neck; and I rejoined the party. We laugh about it now but it took me a while to get past the humiliation and focus on what really mattered about that day: I received a sacrament. The day wasn't supposed to be about the dress, although that's what most young girls focus on, myself included. It was about being blessed to receive the Body of Christ, which I could now do every Sunday at Mass.

The experience also taught me never to build up an event too much in my mind. That just sets you up for disappointment. Things rarely go as planned, and happiness is often about managing expectations and having a sense of humor when things go sideways. Always see the glass as half full.

My Catholic faith was important to me from a young age, and it became even stronger during my freshman year of high school, when I landed in the presence of a future saint: Pope John Paul II. The celebrated pontiff came to New York in October of 1979, and I was fortunate enough to be one of 20,000 enthusiastic young Catholics at Madison Square Garden for his youth rally. John Paul was only 58 at the time, the youngest pope since 1846, and he was relatable. He had played soccer as a kid and was a skier, kayaker, guitar player, actor, playwright, theologian, and prolific writer.

Karol Wojtyla's early life had its share of suffering. His mother died when he was eight. When he was 12, his brother died of scarlet fever. His father passed away a few years later. But he took solace in the church. As a seminarian in his native Poland, he reportedly protected many Polish Jews from the Nazis. Known as the "Pope of Peace," he went on to inspire the formation of the Solidarity movement that ultimately led to the end of Poland's Communist regime. His visit to New York was said to have energized the Catholic Church in America. It certainly energized me. His speech included these words:

> *"This is the meaning of life: to know Christ. To know Christ as a friend…as someone who cares about you and the person next to you, and all the people here and everywhere—no matter what language they speak, or what clothes they wear, or what color their skin is…."*

> *"Because actions speak louder than words, you are called to proclaim, by the conduct of your daily lives, that you really do believe that Jesus Christ is Lord!"*

When Pope John Paul II was canonized in 2014, it made me feel even more blessed to have been there, several decades earlier, when this future saint inspired an arena packed with young Catholics.

It's possible that I knew another future saint as well. In 1986, NYPD officer Steven McDonald was shot in the line of duty by a 15-year-old he was questioning about a stolen bike. Steven was left paralyzed from the neck down. A few months later, he announced that he had forgiven the teen who had confined him to a wheelchair, and he started corresponding with the boy in prison.

My cousin Kevin is married to Steven's sister. A devoted husband and father, Steven refused to succumb to bitterness or despair. Saying anger is a wasted emotion, he spread his message of forgiveness over the next three decades, speaking at high schools, police academies, and even hot spots around the world such as Israel, Northern Ireland, and Bosnia. A devout Catholic, he met three popes, was active in a prayer group, and maintained a devotion to the Blessed Mother.

In the years since Steven's death in 2017, many people whose lives were changed by his message of faith and mercy have joined a call to put "God's Cop" on the path to sainthood. I hope this happens for the man referred to as a "prophet of peace."

CHAPTER 3

The Jigsaw Puzzle

As a new freshman at Saint Francis Prep, the largest Catholic high school in the country, I was interested in joining the track team and the drama club, but both met daily, so I had to choose. I chose track since I was already a runner. I enjoyed the practices and meets, and I met some nice kids, but for some reason I didn't feel a strong connection to the team.

I had looked forward to high school as a fresh start and was hopeful that I would finally "fit in." But so far, that wasn't happening. High school wasn't turning out to be as awesome as I had expected.

Then something wonderful happened. Halfway through freshman year, I was struck with a severe case of scarlet fever.

That was awful, of course, but I truly believe everything happens for a reason. One thing leads to another, and in this case, a horrible illness changed my life for the better.

My sisters and I all got the fever that year, complete with very high temperatures and a pervasive, itchy red rash. On a scale of one to 50, the doctor told my mom my case was a 49. He said if not for penicillin, and based on the severity of my symptoms, I would've died. Thanks to modern medicine, the illness wasn't pretty, but I recovered just fine.

Since permanent vision problems are a risk after scarlet fever, the doctor said I had to wear sunglasses for a while to protect my eyes, even indoors. It was embarrassing walking through the halls of my school looking like an Audrey Hepburn-wannabe. And one older teacher, recalling how deadly scarlet fever used to be, suggested that maybe I should burn my books and desk. (This was not necessary.)

But the main issue was that I was prohibited from running for a few months. No more track.

Oh well; this was my chance to try the drama club. I auditioned for the musical *Bye Bye Birdie*. Just a freshman, I was in the chorus but with a small speaking part. I played "Ursula," a huge fan who swoons over "Conrad Birdie" when the rock star comes to her town. The singing and acting were fun, but the best part was the people!

I got along really well with the other students in the cast. I connected with them instantly and looked forward to rehearsal every day in a way I had never looked forward to track. The cast parties were the highlight of my year, and there was no question that I would continue with drama club the following year, never returning to track. Thanks to a severe illness, I had found my "home" at the school.

I also somehow got elected president of the freshman class. When I was nominated, I thought it was some sort of cruel joke. But it wasn't. My classmates saw something in me that I didn't yet see in myself.

I learned a lot about life in high school, and much of it wasn't on the syllabus. I learned that God has a plan. I was so miserable when I was sick with scarlet fever and so embarrassed to come back wearing those stupid sunglasses. I remember thinking, "Why me?" But what seemed like one of the worst things that had ever happened to me turned out to be one of the best. It led me to my lifelong friends.

I also learned that it's okay to be different. Years later, when I was a semi-famous anchor at News 12 Long Island, I made regular public appearances. One was giving the graduation address at a Catholic grammar school. I saved the speech. It's geared toward kids starting high school, but I think it still holds up. Here's part of it:

When I interview famous people, I usually ask them: What was the secret to your success? And almost all successful people tell me the same thing: They were misfits when they were younger.

It's funny, because I was the same way. I listened to my parents and followed the rules. I was respectful to adults. I studied and did well in school. For some reason, the qualities that make you successful as an adult can be considered negatives in high school. Other kids my age were bending the rules and pushing back against authority. I was labelled a "goody two shoes" or an "egghead."

There's a lot of pressure in high school. Pressure to smoke, to do drugs, to cut class, to do things with the opposite sex that you're not ready to do. I felt all those pressures. I didn't give in. And taking the road less traveled, as the poet Robert Frost said, has made all the difference.

The most important piece of advice I can give you as you head off to high school is to hold on to your individuality.

Teenagers are insecure. Many are scared to stand on their own two feet for fear of being rejected. So they stay in that safe little huddle, laughing when everyone else laughs. The goal is to be inconspicuous. To fit in. That's a strange goal, isn't it? To be like everyone else? When you get older, you realize it's good to be different.

The world is a huge jigsaw puzzle, and each person is a piece. No two pieces are alike, and each one is essential to the whole picture. It doesn't make sense to try to cram a puzzle piece into the wrong space. You just end up damaging that piece. This is foolishness. There is another piece that fits properly there, and that first piece is needed elsewhere. What good is it to have two pieces molded to fit the same space, and nothing left for another space? The whole picture is compromised when we try to force things where they don't belong.

In the same way, we should never change ourselves to conform to anyone else, or push ourselves to act a certain way that isn't right for us. We have a purpose in this life and a responsibility to grow into the people we were destined to become. If we distort our self-image, we eventually can't even recognize our true purpose, just as that puzzle piece will become too distorted to fit into that space where it really belonged.

And you might feel like you're alone in your views, but you're probably not. Chances are there's at least one other person around who feels the same way you do about something. And they would be so relieved if you would put it into words.

As Barry Manilow suggests in his song "I Made It Through the Rain," if you hold on to your unique point of view, when you get older you'll encounter other people who pushed through similar struggles, and you'll all be glad you did. It gets better.

Be true to yourself. And God bless you.

Despite my well-earned reputation as a rule-follower, my twin sister and I did increase our street cred one day in high school by pulling a prank. People frequently asked us if we ever switched places in class, pretending to be each other. We did it once in grammar school, and everyone got a kick out of it. So it seemed inevitable that we would try it at Prep.

With our parents' permission, on April Fool's Day, Colleen attended all of my classes, and I attended hers. We took notes for each other so we could brief each other on what we missed. It all went smoothly for me, but Colleen had some trouble in my biology class.

Mr. Crivelli, who I thought didn't know me from a hole in the wall, sensed that the girl in my seat wasn't me. Colleen still doesn't know how he could tell. She hadn't been called on, so it wasn't her voice. She was just sitting there listening, taking notes. She thinks maybe her posture was different. I think she probably looked too attentive. My teachers always told my parents that they initially thought I wasn't paying attention. I was always staring at my pen or out the window. But when my teachers would try to surprise me by asking what they just taught, I was able to repeat the whole lesson back to them. Eventually they realized I just had a strange way of listening.

Anyway, Colleen says Mr. Crivelli turned to write something on the board, then paused, put down the chalk, spun around and stared at her. He declared, "I think someone's playing an April Fool's joke on me."

He pointed his finger. "You're not Patti Ann!"

Colleen chuckled and said, "You caught me! It's Colleen. April Fool's!"

Everyone laughed. That is, everyone except Mr. Crivelli, who bellowed, "That's not funny! Patti Ann is cutting my class."

The smile wiped off her face, Colleen stammered, "But she's attending *my* biology class, and I'm taking notes for her."

He responded, "None of that matters! She's supposed to be *here*, in my class, right now. She's not. That's cutting! I'm reporting her to the principal. She's getting detention."

In the principal's office, the dean told both of us, "Personally, I think it's hilarious! But technically, Mr. Crivelli is correct. Patti Ann did cut his class, so she has to sit in detention for four days after school."

Since none of Colleen's teachers chose to "press charges," she was off the hook. So she offered to impersonate me again and take two of my four days' detention. I said no. "The madness has to stop! I'm going straight!"

I did the four days and felt like quite the rebel, hanging with the smokers and the truants. It was the only time I was ever "in trouble" at school.

As for Mr. Crivelli, he was honestly one of my favorite teachers. And I must admit I was a bit flattered that he knew that the girl at my desk that day wasn't me. I guess he *did* know me from a hole in the wall.

Being a twin was certainly fun at times. The best part was having a best friend who was my age, going through the same things I was going through. Colleen always had my back, and I had hers. But it also had its drawbacks.

For starters, it was difficult for our sister, Mary Lou. She was less than a year younger than us, so theoretically, all three of us should have been close friends. But three is not a good number.

Colleen and I were born first, and sonograms show that twins start to bond even before birth. So we became pals in the womb and got even more attached during our first year. By the time Mary Lou came along, we didn't need her, and we were oblivious to the fact that she needed us. We also didn't appreciate having to share our mother's attention with another baby. Looking back, we were pretty heartless when it came to our younger sister. Kids are really stupid.

Mary Lou was jealous of our bond. Since kids don't understand human nature, she expressed her jealousy by relentlessly tormenting both of us. Colleen and I were always mad at Mary Lou for doing mean things to us behind our parents' backs.

We'd complain to our mom, and she'd say, "Mary Lou just wants to be your friend." We had to repeatedly explain to our obviously clueless mother that Mary Lou *hated* us. Meanwhile, Mary Lou would complain that we were always making it "two against one."

This vicious cycle continued for many years. If we went to the amusement park, it was assumed that Colleen and I would ride the two-seat rides together. Mary Lou would have to find someone else. In our house, Colleen and I shared a room, while Mary Lou was alone. It's easy to see now that my mom was right: Mary Lou was acting out of hurt.

As we got older, it changed. Mary Lou got the scarlet fever before I did, and I was deeply troubled by how weak she looked.

She was scared, and I was scared for her. I realized how much I loved her.

By high school, we were all able to see more clearly how the randomness of birth order can have profound effects on sibling relations. The three of us worked it out, and we've all been best friends ever since. Mary Lou lives five blocks away from me, and it's great being close to her and her family. Colleen lives about an hour away, and we talk and text daily. My two sisters are among my greatest gifts in life.

But another drawback of being a twin is obvious. People couldn't tell Colleen and me apart. Although the doctor who delivered us said we were "fraternal" twins, we looked identical. Often, people didn't even bother trying to distinguish between us. We stopped dressing alike and made a point of having different hairstyles, but people lumped us together as "The Browne Twins," as if it really didn't matter which one was which. People rarely said my name in high school. Not knowing which twin I was, they greeted me with "Yo!" or "Hey Brownie!"

Some would come up with unflattering ways to tell us apart.

"Your cheeks are chubbier," was something I heard often, while Colleen got tired of people pointing out a tiny scar on her cheek.

We were both also asked, "Which one is the smart one and which is the popular one?" We got the message. Only one of us could be smart and one could be popular. We could not be both.

It was impossible not to compare us. If Colleen accomplished something, I had no excuse for not being able to do the same thing. When she first dove off the high board at the pool, I felt sick. I could *jump* off that board but was terrified of diving after witnessing someone's painful belly flop. But now that Colleen had gone off head first, I would have to do the same. If she could do it, I had no excuse. We were the same age, had the same build, the same training. The only difference was that I didn't have her courage.

In retrospect, it was a good thing. She pushed me to do things that were out of my comfort zone merely by doing them herself. She was my guinea pig. She survived diving off the high board, and soon enough, so did I.

When we were both running track, it was a strange mix of competitiveness and support. If Colleen was ahead of me in a race, I berated myself for being slower than she was. I could rationalize losing to the other runners. They were taller or had springier ankles. None of that applied to Colleen. We were twins. Curse her for making me look bad.

But if I was ahead of her in a race, I spent all my time worrying about why she wasn't keeping up. *Is she hurt? Should I slow down and check on her? She must feel so bad about my beating her. I feel so guilty.* Yep, being a twin is a head trip.

Then there was the drama club. After Colleen saw what a great time I had doing *Bye Bye Birdie*, she joined the club with me in our sophomore year. When we were juniors, she got the main role we both auditioned for in the musical. I stayed in the chorus.

I developed a big crush on one of the drama club guys. One night at a party, I was thrilled when he asked me to take a walk with him. Then he turned to me nervously and said, "I want to ask you… how to win your twin sister's heart."

It was a major bummer at the time, but a psychologist might say these experiences sparked my desire to be recognized, which motivated me to pursue a career on the air. And that worked out pretty well, so maybe it all happened for a reason.

Overall, my high school years were great. In addition to track and drama club, I was also a retreat leader and involved in campus ministries. I made National Honor Society in my junior and senior years, and danced in Prep's 24-hour dance-a-thon for charity.

For spending money, I babysat and worked at McDonald's. The franchise I worked at had an indoor playroom, and I mainly worked as a kids' party hostess. Since I got tips, it was usually a pretty good gig. But the kids would stuff their faces with a burger, fries, and a large shake, and then spin as fast as possible on the ill-conceived indoor spinning ride. Inevitably, at least one child would end up depositing their barely digested Happy Meal on our tacky green carpet. I had to mop it up. On those days, I definitely felt I earned my tips!

I spent my earnings on nights out with my friends. We also had some great parties in our wood-paneled basement. We were given an awesome used jukebox by one of my dad's business associates whose kids were big music buffs. The jukebox was stocked with great 45s (single-song records) from the 1960s and early '70s. Back then, our friends thought it was insanely cool that they could "play DJ" by programming whatever songs they liked into the jukebox. (We disabled the coin slot, of course.) By the way, the daughter of the couple who gave us the jukebox, Kim Ashley, has been a big-time radio DJ for decades. Thanks for the 45s, Kim!

Always a music fan, for a year or two I was the singer in a basement band with some high school friends. The band was called "Blacklist" and I mainly sang covers of songs by Pat Benatar and the Go-Go's. We practiced at the drummer's house and played a few gigs, including Mary Lou's Sweet 16 party in our backyard. But then we all went off to college, and the band broke up. I wasn't a great singer, but it was fun to "live the dream" for a short time.

Plus, I felt it would benefit me to attend a different college from Colleen. We were very attached, and I knew we would miss each other terribly, but I felt I needed to break away and establish an identity apart from hers.

So I told my parents I wanted to go to Fordham. But my mom had taken a job at a well-regarded nearby university, specifically for the free tuition offered to employees' families. The plan was for all three of us to go there.

If I had my heart set on Fordham, I could still go there if I got a scholarship. That was fair. My mom's secretarial job didn't pay much. The whole point was to cover the three tuitions. So I hit the books hard. I spent a lot of time doing practice college entrance exams.

I was also experiencing the usual stress of high school. Being a teenager induces anxiety, and I was the sensitive type. I guess the pressure finally got to me.

One weekend, I was in my room in the middle of the day and felt the need to lie down on top of my bed. The next thing I knew, hours had passed, and my mom was yelling up the stairs to say dinner was ready. I woke up, sat up, and blacked out. Once the furniture in my room gradually came back into view, I stood up and felt very dizzy.

I made my way slowly down the stairs and wobbled into the kitchen. My family, already seated, was giving me funny looks. My mom said, "Patti Ann, you look green."

I passed out again and was dragged to the couch. I came to, and my mom and dad were yelling, "What's wrong? Wake up!"

They say when people are bleeding internally, they often say, "I'm dying." And they're not wrong. Internal bleeding literally drains your life blood away from your organs, eventually killing you.

I also got to dance on TV. During my senior year, one of my drama club friends invited my high school gang to be on a new syndicated dance show called *We're Dancin'*. She had a connection in the industry. The show was similar to *American Bandstand*. People danced to new wave music in a brightly-lit studio.

The show included live performances. The episode I was on featured Billy Idol and the Stray Cats. I was chosen to ask Billy a question on air after one of his songs. The host, Townsend Coleman, angled his mic to me so I could ask Billy, "What made you decide to put your album *White Wedding* on a white disc?"

Billy responded in his sexy British accent, "We wanted it to be on virgin vinyl."

Everyone oohed and aahed. Come to think of it, I guess that was my television debut and my first time conducting an on-air "interview."

The show only lasted one season. I'm sure my dancing didn't help. When my episode aired on Channel 5 (New York's Fox broadcast station), I was horrified.

"*That's* what I look like when I dance?!"

After that, I referred to the show as *Weird Dancing*. And here I had been thinking I'd be discovered and cast on the TV series *Fame*.

That same year, I got my driver's license. Literally weeks later, I was finishing up my shift at McDonald's when my boss, Kathleen, complained that it had started snowing. She had walked to work. But I had my car! (Okay, it was my parents' car.) I offered to drive her home, and off we went.

The snow was coming down, and the roads had not been plowed, but it was a very short trip, and I was driving cautiously, so what could go wrong? Well, as we approached a red traffic light,

I tapped the brakes. The car did not respond on the slippery road. It was my first time driving in snow, and I was unfamiliar with this scenario, so now I slammed the brakes. This, of course, caused the car to skid. Luckily, I was going extremely slowly, but the car ever-so-gently slid forward on the new-fallen snow, gliding to a stop when it tapped the bumper of the car stopped in front of us at the light—an NYPD squad car.

"Oh my God, you just hit a cop car!" my boss noted helpfully.

The police car rocked slightly, and I could see the officer inside looking in his rearview mirror to figure out what had just happened.

He stepped out and approached my car, looking more puzzled than angry. There was zero damage to either car, but…*who would hit a cop car?*

"License and registration, please," he ordered as I rolled down my window and started apologizing profusely.

"I hit the brakes, but the car didn't stop!"

"Have you been drinking?" he asked.

"No! I'm coming from work."

Kathleen backed me up. "Officer, I'm her boss and we just finished our shift, and she was driving me home because it's snowing."

Examining my ID, he said with surprise, "You just got this license."

"Yes," I said. "I'm a brand new driver. The brakes didn't work!"

"Have you ever driven in snow before?"

"No."

"It takes practice. You can't slam the brakes. You have to keep tapping them. You'll figure it out. Are you going straight home now?"

Kathleen jumped out of the car and said, "Yes, I'll walk from here!"

Reading my address on the license, the officer said, "" just two blocks away."

"Yes," I said, "I'm right down this street."

He said, "Go straight home, and practice braking in snc parking lot when you can."

"I will! Thank you!"

When I arrived home, my mom asked, "How was work?"

Ashamed and embarrassed, I replied, "Work was fine."

It wasn't a lie. Work *had* been fine. I just neglected to me the little incident that happened *after* work.

New drivers really do learn as they go, and I feel lucky tha was my only mishap. I was also very grateful to this cop for b so understanding. As with so many things in life, it could've I much worse.

By senior year of high school, I had my heart set on Fordh University in the Bronx. It had a beautiful campus, great Je professors, and I really loved the college radio station. WFUV-I runs an Irish music show every Sunday that my dad listened to r giously. I always dreamed I would one day be on that show.

I also saw myself anchoring radio news. My mom says th when I was four, I was chatting with her on a city bus. A man ne to us commented that he was a teacher and that I spoke better age four than his students did in junior high. I would also bore th family during breakfast by reading the writing on the cereal box ou loud, including the ingredients. Once, my sisters and I, along with neighbor, Patty, did a pretend "show" in which I interviewed them with a hose. So Fordham, with its strong communications program seemed ideal for my career goals.

As I lay on the couch with my parents' blurry faces coming in and out of focus, I knew I was in big trouble.

I grabbed my mom's arm and said weakly but urgently, "Help me."

"What do you need me to do?!" she asked in a panic.

At a loss, I said I felt like I needed to go to the bathroom, so my mom helped me there.

My dad found himself saying, "Don't flush!"

He had read something about stool color and internal bleeding, and God planted that thought in his head at just the right time.

Sure enough, it was black—a sign of bleeding.

My parents rushed me to the hospital. I drifted in and out of consciousness the whole way there.

At the emergency room, my parents each took an armpit and pulled me to the desk. My head dropped onto the counter with a thud. The receptionist picked up my head and asked, "WHAT DID YOU TAKE?"

Confused, I replied, "What?"

"WHAT DRUG DID YOU TAKE?" she asked, still gripping my head in both of her hands and looking me right in the eyes, which were rolling around in my head.

"Nothing," I said feebly.

"ARE YOU PREGNANT?!" (I still can't figure out how my symptoms suggested pregnancy, but apparently when a teenage girl enters the ER they assume it's either drugs or pregnancy.)

I assured her there was no possibility of that, and she told me to take a seat. We waited while other people were treated ahead of me. I sat slumped in my chair, feeling myself slipping away, thinking I was not going to make it. My dad finally marched back to the desk and handed the woman a Tupperware containing my, um, handiwork from the toilet.

One peek and the receptionist immediately called for a wheelchair, and I was rushed to the back. Tests on the sample confirmed internal bleeding. My dad's quick thinking had saved my life. God had whispered a thought in his head at just the right time, and he had listened.

I was given a transfusion of two pints of blood, which only replaced some of what I had lost. While new blood was coming into me through a vein, old blood was coming out through a tube shoved up my nose and down to my torso. Apparently, the blood I had lost was swimming around in my abdomen. It was now being vacuumed out through the tube and into a large basin on my lap. The first basin filled up and had to be replaced with a second. I realized this had been a very close call.

Once I was stable and settled into a hospital bed, the questions started again. The main one was still, "What drugs are you on?"

I was able to establish that I had never taken any illegal drugs, but I did drink beer. (Times were different then. I was 17, the drinking age was 18, and most of my friends were a year or two older than me.) I had been at a party drinking the night before, but a battery of tests determined that alcohol wasn't the cause of my internal bleeding.

It was an ulcer. So now the questions changed. *Are you under a lot of pressure? Do you have a lot of anxiety? Do you get bad grades?* At some point, I told them I was a straight A student, and I was studying for a scholarship.

Ah! So it's her parents' fault....

They found my distraught mom and dad in the hall and explained that their poor daughter almost died of a bleeding duodenal ulcer because they were putting too much pressure on her and making her study for a scholarship.

Back in my room, I was just grateful to be alive and grateful to my parents for saving me. They came into the room and, to my surprise, my mom burst into tears and said, "We're so sorry! You can go to any college you want to go to!"

Um, what?

My parents again apologized profusely for almost killing me by encouraging me to study for the SAT.

Man, what did I miss? I'm so confused. I must still be delirious.

I assured them that the pressure I felt was self-imposed. And it wasn't even that bad. If anything, the other stresses of high school were weighing on me more. And, let's face it, the beer I drank the night before probably didn't help. But my near-death experience had changed everything.

They insisted, "Don't worry about a scholarship. We can pay for it. We just need to shuffle things around. Go to Fordham. Pursue your dream."

I was hospitalized for a week, and I left with a new diet and medication regimen and more importantly, a new attitude.

The ulcer eventually healed. And despite pulling back on the studying to recover, I did well on the SAT, got some scholarship money, and the following fall I was a Fordham Ram (or, technically, a Ewe).

I don't recommend internal bleeding, but I must say…coming that close to dying really does put things in perspective. I realized I needed to learn to shrug things off, to keep working on that sense of humor, and to stop sweating the small stuff. Stress can literally kill you.

And I realized something else. *This was one of the rainy days my parents had been saving for.* My parents had always known things would come up. This was one. It taught me the importance of being careful with my money.

I also realized I needed more faith. I had made it through the rain again. God works in strange ways. Sometimes our worst experiences are blessings in disguise.

CHAPTER 4

Doors

"Put it out there in the universe…
Take chances. Do things that you've dreamed
of doing. Get out of your comfort zone."

–JANICE DEAN, *MOSTLY SUNNY: HOW I LEARNED TO*
KEEP SMILING THROUGH THE RAINIEST DAYS

"This is a compact disc," the DJ told me excitedly in our radio studio, holding up a flat, shiny object. "It holds 80 minutes of music!"

The DJ was Lou Rufino, who went on to be the well-known engineer for shock jock radio host Don Imus. The studio was at WFUV, Fordham University's highly-regarded radio station.

As soon as I started at Fordham, I signed up to be a news anchor for this student-run station, and I spent most of my free time in its dingy corridors on the third floor of Keating Hall.

The walls of the station were lined with well-worn record albums stacked from floor to ceiling. The studio had several turntables but it had also recently acquired a new device called a CD player.

Compact discs had come out the prior year, but they weren't widely circulated. I had never seen one until that day in 1983. How could they fit so much music on such a small disc? And how was it possible that you could play the songs out of order? Lou explained that it had to do with lasers, and you didn't even need a needle to play it. It was one of the many small things that made my time at WFUV exciting.

The lack of CDs at our radio station was less remarkable than the fact that we had no computers. Back then, we got our news from an Associated Press (AP) machine in a closet in the back of the newsroom. Called a "wire machine" because it originally received stories transmitted over telegraph wires, it was essentially a teletype printer that spat out news copy on rolls of paper. We would rip the stories "off the wire" and use them as source material for our newscasts, which we banged out on noisy manual typewriters. (I think by my senior year, we had upgraded to electric typewriters.) If news broke too late to rewrite, we would "rip and read," sprinting into the studio to deliver the scoop live from the AP into the big foam-covered microphones.

We recorded field interviews on portable tape recorders, and sound bites were dubbed onto boxy cartridges known as "carts." Similar to 8-track cassettes, carts held short amounts of audio, and if they played out, they re-cued to the beginning. If you stopped them in the middle during your newscast, it was essential that you "re-cue your carts" later or risk getting chewed out by the next shift.

Longer audio was recorded onto reels with thin audiotape wound around them. Editing meant loading the reel onto one side of a machine and wrapping the start of the tape around an empty reel next to it. The tape between the two sides was pulled onto a "play head." We would manually "rock the reels" back and forth to listen for the edit point as it crossed the play head. Then we'd mark that point on the tape with a wax pencil, cut it with a razor blade, and tape the two sides back together again with skinny splicing tape. The piece we cut out fell to the "cutting room floor"—an expression still used today, though many young people don't know why.

I loved editing reels. (And, apparently, they're coming back in vogue.) I also loved reading the wire and feeling like the first person to know about a big story. I loved the challenge of writing short, clear newscasts. And I loved diving into the world of current events. Back then, I had a lot to learn about news, and I did my best to get up to speed.

During my freshman and sophomore years, I wrote and anchored short newscasts for WFUV on a regular basis. Eventually, I was anchoring the half-hour roundup called *Special Report*. My sports anchor for that newscast was often Bob Papa, now a New York Giants play-by-play and NBC Olympics announcer, and sometimes Jack Curry, now a New York Yankees analyst.

In my junior year, I was named News Director—a position I held until I graduated. It was my first time in a managerial position, and I discovered I needed to work on my people skills. I had plenty of time to do that, since WFUV did not shut down over the summers. While other students stayed home for summer vacation, I spent a few nights each week in a free dorm provided by Fordham so I could run WFUV's news department and anchor lots of newscasts. I wasn't alone. I had the company of a small, dedicated team of classmates who shared my love of all things radio.

I didn't just love news. I loved everything about the radio environment. I loved being able to pull out an album and listen to "deep cuts." I loved hearing about all the latest bands from our very knowledgeable student DJs. I loved learning how to use the "patch panel" and the audio board (thank you, Rich Tammero). And I loved the unique variety of programs our station aired.

As a junior, I was named co-host of the famed WFUV Sunday Irish show. Called *Ceol na Gael,* Gaelic for "music of the Irish" (they've since added an "n" before the "G"), this show was almost considered "required listening" for Irish families in the Bronx and some other parts of the New York metro area, including Connecticut.

Unlike most college radio stations, WFUV's frequency, 90.7 FM, was not limited to the campus. It was a full 50,000 watts—the same power as the major commercial radio stations. WFUV was, and still is, a college radio powerhouse.

I was out of my depth as an Irish show host. My co-host, Kathleen Biggins, was extremely well-versed in Irish music and culture, and was kind enough to show me the ropes. But I still cringe when I play old cassette tapes of my radio shows. I had a Queens accent, I made lots of mistakes, and I just generally sounded like an amateur. But I guess that's what a college radio station is for.

I hosted the Irish show for two years, and it was a great experience. The show had a 1.6 Arbitron rating—a huge number for a college radio station at the time—and raised $80,000 in its fundraising telethon. Kathleen and I were invited to see all the hot Irish bands, and we were guests at local *ceilis* and *feises* (Irish dance parties and competitions). I spent some weekends in East Durham, an area of the Catskill Mountains sometimes referred to as "Ireland's 33rd County." I was treated to bagpipe music at a Hamptons barbecue hosted by Kevin McCarthy of the NYPD Emerald Society Pipe and Drum Band. We regularly interviewed Irish American politicians like Nassau County Comptroller Peter King (later a US Congressman for decades).

One day, a new record landed on our desk at the station. It was "The Irish Wedding Song," written by Ian Betteridge and recorded by a young new Irish American artist named Andy Cooney. We played it, and it quickly became a top request on our show, as well as a staple at Irish weddings.

One Sunday, we interviewed Andy live in our studio. After that, he and I dated briefly. One of our dates was a Phil Coulter concert at Carnegie Hall. Sitting in the audience, Andy turned to me and said, "One day, I'll be singing on that stage, and you'll be a network news anchor."

I chuckled and said, "Absolutely!" But at the time, it seemed like a pipe dream.

Fast-forward about 20 years.... An invitation arrived for my husband and me to a concert at Carnegie Hall, headlined by my old friend Andy Cooney. At the time, I was an anchor for Fox News Channel. I remembered young Andy's prediction and smiled. As my friend Janice Dean observes in her inspiring memoir, sometimes you just have to put your dreams out into the universe. Visualize it, believe it, and, most importantly, work for it.

While heavily involved in WFUV's news department, I also worked part-time at *Newsweek* all through college. Starting my freshman year, I would take the D-train from Fordham into Manhattan twice a week, to the Madison Avenue offices of this weekly magazine. I worked in the photo department and had no involvement in editorial matters, but I learned a lot and got paid to do it.

One of the things I learned is that news can break at inconvenient times. There were days when the whole magazine was ready to print but had to be ripped apart when a big story hit. In 1984, Indian Prime Minister Indira Gandhi was assassinated at about 11 PM (New York time). Obviously, that became our new cover story, and everything else had to be moved around.

I would work till 4 AM on days like that. *Newsweek* would put us up at the Intercontinental Hotel to catch a few hours' sleep, and then we'd come back later that morning to finish the job. I remember laying my head on the hotel pillow and getting a wake-up call what seemed like mere minutes later. When I finally made it back to my Fordham dorm, I'd sleep most of Saturday. I missed out on a lot of college socializing. It was an early glimpse of the brutal hours in the news business. But I kept the job for four years. I loved the atmosphere.

Over the summers, I had other jobs too. One was waitressing at a country club on Long Island's north shore. Another was teaching aerobics. But my favorite summer job during college was at Shea Stadium, where the New York Mets played before Citi Field opened. For two summers, when I wasn't at the radio station, I was there selling hot dogs and beer from behind the counter. (Girls were not allowed to work the stands back then.) The tips were great when the Mets were winning. When they were losing, the lines were long, and the customers were in bad moods.

Luckily, the Mets were winning a lot. I worked there in 1986, the year the Mets won the World Series. (I was back at school during the series itself and cheered on the team in a dorm with fellow Met fans.) The job at Shea was far from glamorous, but it was awesome to be there during the years of Keith Hernandez, Darryl Strawberry, Dwight Gooden, and Gary Carter.

It was great to be earning my own money. Between *Newsweek* and my summer jobs, I was able to save enough to travel to London with some high school friends during a college recess. We visited our friend Joe Peiser, who was studying at Oxford. Our group included his future wife Andrea, my sister Colleen, and lifelong friend Mark Reisig. The exchange rate back then was highly favorable to Americans, and we soaked up all the sights.

The following year, I flew to Hungary during a break to visit Colleen, who was spending a semester studying abroad in Budapest. We also visited Vienna and Salzburg, Austria. Those trips were a lot of fun, and seeing other countries really does broaden one's perspective.

I also went to the Bahamas for spring break during my senior year. That wasn't quite as educational, but my friend Joanne and I had a good time.

Throughout college, I still hung out a lot with my high school gang, even though we were at different colleges. We all went home to Queens during breaks and over the summer, so we played co-ed flag football in the park and hung out at some local watering holes.

I dated a little in college but had no serious boyfriends. I mingled with Fordham classmates at the two off-campus bars, Clarke's and the Lantern. (Again, the drinking age was lower back then.) But since I was hosting the Irish show every Sunday, Saturday night couldn't be too crazy. Kathleen and I would get to the station at 10:30 AM to prep for our 12:30 show. That doesn't sound terribly early, but for college students, it seemed like an ungodly hour of the morning. And the show was three-and-a-half hours long, so it was best not to have a hangover.

I was also co-editor of Fordham's literary magazine, *Alternative Motifs*, for a year. And I interned for ABC News anchor Joan Lunden on her syndicated talk show about parenting, called *Mother's Day*, produced by her then-husband, Michael Krauss.

Between the radio station, the job, and my other activities, I was pretty busy. But I made Dean's List my freshman year and maintained good grades for all four years at Fordham, earning a Bachelor of Arts degree in Communications.

The summer after graduation, Colleen and I spent a month traveling around Ireland and France. Since we paid for the trip with our own money, we were on a budget, so we took trains everywhere and walked a lot. In Ireland, we visited relatives and heard fascinating stories about our ancestors.

My dad's family is mainly from Mayo, so while visiting that county, we stayed with his relatives, Edie and Mickey Loftus. Better known as Dr. Michael Loftus, Uncle Mickey is well-known in Ireland. He was on the Mayo team that won the All-Ireland Senior Gaelic Football Championship in 1951, which is a very big deal over there. He went on to become the influential president of the Gaelic Athletic Association.

Uncle Mickey and Aunt Edie and their kids were gracious hosts, and they told us so many things we didn't know about our grandparents and other relatives. Their son Michael and his wife, Eleanor, took us sailing off Achill Island. Ireland might be even more beautiful from the water. We still stay in touch with all the Loftuses and get together when in each other's countries.

My mom's family tree centers on Donegal. It's a beautiful county with a rocky coastline featuring breathtaking views of the Atlantic Ocean. Our relatives there were warm and welcoming.

Colleen and I took a train to Ireland's east coast to see U2 playing at Croke Park in Dublin. The Pretenders opened for them. It was the best concert I've ever attended.

Then we ferried across to France and spent some time in Paris. We dined outdoors on the Left Bank, saw the Mona Lisa at the Louvre, and admired Notre Dame Cathedral decades before it was damaged by fire. It was a great trip and a wonderful way to close one chapter of my life and begin another.

So now what? I knew I loved broadcasting, but I had attended several career talks by veteran newscasters who warned that the stress of this industry invariably led to high blood pressure, chain smoking, and divorce. I wanted marriage and stability. It seemed like an either/or situation.

So, I decided to abandon my dream of being a news anchor. Since I had enjoyed my four years at *Newsweek*, I figured I could have a good life working for a magazine.

I took a job with a woman's magazine that's no longer in existence. My goal was to write and edit articles, but the entry-level job available was in ad sales. I was assured that once in-house, I could make the switch from advertising to editorial. Young and naïve, I didn't realize that was a crock of you-know-what.

I did not enjoy my time in ad sales. At one point, I was in our publisher's office (we'll call her "Susan") when she took a call from an underling and started ripping into her, finally yelling, "I feel like killing you!"

Wow. This was not the supportive all-female environment I had hoped for. Despite being unhappy, I worked hard and was soon offered a small promotion. The supervisor offering me the advancement could see I was ambivalent, so she gave me what she thought was the ultimate enticement: "You could be the next Susan!"

Well that did it. The thought of becoming the next Susan was actually my ultimate nightmare. The overall women's magazine culture just didn't feel like a good fit for me. Besides, I never wanted to be in ad sales. I wanted to write my own stories.

Taking the train home to my parents' house where I was still living, I tried to figure out how to break it to them that I wanted to quit my first real job after just a few months.

I expected them to be disappointed. When we're young, we're taught not to be quitters. We're taught to follow through on our commitments. This ethic gets confusing once we begin our working lives. It feels wrong to quit a job, even if we're miserable. Our bosses are "authority figures," and we're supposed to do what they say. Quitting feels disloyal to our employer, who was gracious enough to give us this job we applied for. We're also admitting we made a mistake.

That's not how my parents saw it.

"That's great!" they exclaimed.

"Mom, Dad, do you understand that I have no job lined up? You'll have to support me while I figure out what I'm going to do for a living now."

"Obviously you'll pursue your true passion—broadcast news!" my dad said.

"But what about the horrible hours, the skipped meals, the deadlines, the ulcer?" I replied.

"Patti Ann, you'll make it work. You have to follow your heart. It's obvious you love broadcasting. It's what you were born to do."

They were right. The fact is "adulting" means taking control of your own life and not allowing yourself to be pushed in directions you don't want to go.

And if you make a choice and realize it was wrong, you have to make a correction—the sooner, the better. If you figure out you're climbing up the wrong ladder, start climbing down! If you keep climbing up that ladder, thinking it's right to "stay the course," you'll just have a longer, more difficult trip back down once you inevitably realize you don't want what's waiting for you at the top of that ladder.

It felt weird going into my boss's office the next day and giving her my notice. She was my boss, but once I told her I was quitting, I felt the power shift. I was in charge. And I should be in charge. This is *my* life. I get to write my own story.

I warned my parents that it would take me a long time to find a full-time job as a radio newscaster. Those jobs were hard to come by. And in New York, the top radio market in the country, once people got those spots, they kept them forever.

My parents promised to support me. Still, I was starting to panic. They wouldn't take care of me forever. Obviously, I needed a job. I barely knew where to begin.

One week after I left the magazine, I was named full-time news anchor for WLIM-AM, a small radio station in Suffolk County, Long Island, that played big-band classics.

It happened much faster than I expected.

"Nature loves courage," lecturer Terence McKenna said in his speech, "Unfolding the Stone."

"You make the commitment and nature will respond to that commitment by removing impossible obstacles."

This quote rings so true to me.

Back then there was no internet. People read about job openings in the classified ads. So, once I quit my job, I purchased the latest issue of *Broadcasting Magazine*. Having glanced at this national industry periodical in the past, I knew there was almost never a listing in my area. But what the heck, it was a place to start. I figured when that didn't work, I would personally contact the local radio stations and ask if I could get my foot in the door working as a gopher. But when I turned to the magazine's back pages, there it was:

Long Island radio station seeks full-time morning-drive news anchor.

I could not believe my eyes. It was a tiny, obscure station an hour east of my home, but still a place to start for someone like me. Realizing other people were also reading this ad, I knew time was of the essence. I hadn't even updated my resume yet!

Our house only had a typewriter, but my mom used a computer at her job. I hurried to her office, arriving beet red and huffing and puffing. She asked her boss if she could take a half hour. He said yes. She typed up a nice new resume for me, and I rushed it to WLIM in Patchogue.

I was granted an interview, but reviewing my resume, News Director George Drake told me they never hire right out of college. I pointed out that I had four years' experience as a news writer and anchor, and was even a news director. The only difference between a professional and me was the fact that I didn't get paid.

Mr. Drake decided to give me an audition. He handed me a reel and showed me the newsroom, the AP machine, the typewriter, and the studio. He told me to write and record a complete two-minute newscast.

"Start with the call letters, time and temp. Then three stories, one including a sound bite from our affiliate news service." He pointed to a stack of carts on the desk.

"Then sports and weather, then close. Record it and edit it on this reel. The machine is in the studio. The carts for the opening and closing music are in there too."

I smiled. I had literally done this a thousand times at Fordham.

"What's my deadline?"

"Just get it to me as fast as you can." He walked away.

I ripped the wires, chose some stories, and listened to the affiliate packages. I picked a sound bite from one, edited it on the reel-to-reel, and recorded it onto a cart. I typed out a script and brought it into the studio, inserted my carts into the slots, and loaded the reel. I did a sound check and adjusted my levels on the audio board, then recorded the newscast, start to finish. One take.

A short time later, I knocked on Mr. Drake's office door.

I could see from his expression that he thought I was there to concede defeat.

"Yes, do you need help?"

"No, I just wanted to give you the reel."

"You weren't able to do it?"

"Oh, no, I did it. It's on the reel."

"You're *done*?" he asked, clearly impressed.

He told me to wait in a room while he played my reel in the studio.

He came back and told me the job was mine.

Was I lucky? Absolutely! I was blessed to get that opportunity. But it would've been worthless if I hadn't had the skills to back it up. I worked very hard for years so that I could take advantage of any breaks that came my way—not WLIM specifically; I didn't even know that opportunity would exist. But I knew in my gut, all through college, that I had to work my tail off so I'd be ready when my future came knocking.

WLIM was a great first job in broadcasting. Owner/DJ Jack Ellsworth was a legend in the big band world and a much-loved figure on Long Island. He treated his staff like family. His wife,

Dot, popped in frequently. They were a warm, loving couple. Their beautiful golden retriever would wander the halls, bringing smiles to all of us. WLIM's news reporter, Michael Graham, was a great guy—smart, funny, and self-deprecating.

I had to wake up before 4 AM to drive out to Patchogue in the dark, catch up on the news, and deliver it every half hour to morning rush-hour drivers. The upside was that I was done by early afternoon, so I could exercise and take care of household stuff. I liked being a morning person.

But this AM station actually had a lower wattage than my college station, and the pay was very low. I would never be able to move out of my parents' house on that salary. There were no openings at the bigger local radio stations. So, I started to look at TV.

The television landscape was expanding. Cable TV was really taking off, meaning there were now many channels in need of news anchors and reporters—not just the big networks and their affiliates, as had been the case for decades.

But how would I make the jump from radio to television? You couldn't get a job without showing a tape of your previous TV reporting, and you couldn't show your previous reporting unless you already had a TV job.

I couldn't figure out a way around this Catch-22, but I plugged along at WLIM, confident that something, somehow, would change.

One night, I went out with Colleen and a bunch of her old college friends. I ended up chatting with one of them, Mike Clark, who, as of this writing, has been an anchor in Pittsburgh for more than 20 years. It was a chat that would change my life.

Mike was going for his master's degree at the New York Institute of Technology. He explained that NYIT produced a newscast that aired every night on Long Island's religious cable channel, Telecare (now the Catholic Faith Network). Students arrived at the college TV studio in Old Westbury early in the morning. Aspiring reporters were assigned a story and a videographer-in-training. They went out in the field, conducted interviews, shot video, came back to the studio, and produced a story that aired that night on the show, called *L.I. News Tonight*.

Mike insisted that I take a day off from my radio job to follow him around.

After a day of shadowing Mike, watching him create a "package," and seeing it air on cable TV, I was hooked and my path was clear. I would register as a graduate student at the New York Institute of Technology.

But wait…. Now I'd have to take out loans or ask my parents to help me go back to school. Hadn't they done enough? This troubled me, but my parents told me to go ahead and sign up, and I could pay them back later.

It didn't come to that. Thanks to my high grades at Fordham and my radio news experience, I was granted a teacher assistantship—a full scholarship in exchange for helping to teach radio skills to undergrads. My previous hard work was really paying off.

I loved reporting for *L.I. News*. I covered a wide variety of stories, from homicides to traffic problems to property taxes. Very often, I was working side-by-side with reporters for New York City's big stations. These were some of the best reporters in the business. At a press conference, I would pay close attention to the questions they asked. If we were covering a crime scene, I watched how they approached neighbors, police, and victims' relatives. I took note of their choice of standup location, and what "B-roll" (video footage to play under audio tracks) their videographers were shooting. Every night, I would watch their stories on ABC or NBC and compare mine to theirs. Theirs were usually better. But once in a while, I felt that I did a better job conveying the story.

Eventually our news director, Ken Eckhardt, assigned me a "special report." These were 15-minute in-depth pieces. Mine would be my master's thesis. Ken urged me to choose a topic I was passionate about. I chose water pollution.

I worked extremely hard on this report. Our program director, Gary Licker, taught me how to shut off the lights and lock up the newsroom, since I was often in an editing booth well after everyone else was gone for the night, logging my interviews, choosing video, and working on the script. I knew I was going above and beyond what was required, but I was passionate about the topic and really enjoyed this project. I was doing what I loved.

I got an A on my special report and straight As in all my other classes. I ended up with a perfect 4.0 GPA. I enjoyed helping to teach radio production throughout my time as a grad student. And while at NYIT, I also learned how to edit video, roll the prompter, and even took a turn directing a show.

But as my time was wrapping up, the questions started coming.

"What are you going to do now? Do you have a job lined up?"

No, I didn't. And I was too busy to even put together a decent audition tape. I had done a few pieces called *Viacom Community Camera* for Cablevision's TV6. But that wasn't full-time work. I was once again relying on God to provide somehow. But He seemed to be taking His time.

Then, literally weeks before my classes ended, Ken told me he had submitted my special report for a few awards. It had won. In competition with the New York affiliates' Long Island correspondents, my report won the 1st place regional Associated Press award for Documentary Feature, a FOLIO Award (Focus On Long Island Operations), and a Long Island Press Club Award.

The FOLIO awards ceremony was a big event at a fancy hall, attended by all of Long Island's media big wigs and many from the city. People took note of the win by a reporter for a college station.

As the ceremony wound down, I was approached by Marvin Chauvin, who ran TV 55 Long Island. He congratulated me and asked if I could fill in for his news anchor for a few days while she took a short vacation. Um, yes!

It turned out her "vacation" was an audition for a job in a bigger market. She got the job and, within weeks, TV 55 had a full-time vacancy. And just like that, I was a paid, full-time TV news anchor.

That's the thing about opportunities—they can show up when you least expect them. Janice and I both love a quote by author Joseph Campbell: "When you follow your bliss, the universe will open doors where there were only walls."

There was just one problem. I still lived in Queens with my parents, and TV 55 was on Cablevision, which was only available in Nassau and Suffolk. That doesn't seem like a big problem? Tell that to my parents! They were determined to watch their daughter anchoring the news on TV.

There was a possible way. TV 55 was also a broadcast channel, but the signal, coming from Riverhead, barely reached Queens. So, my dad bought an absurdly large antenna and climbed on the roof to install it. He kept yelling down to my mom, "Can you see the picture now?!"

"No!"

"How about now?"

"Still no!"

After experimenting with multiple locations, my parents discovered that the very best signal came with the antenna smack-dab in middle of our living room. I am not exaggerating. It was like an "antenna tree," with metal branches extending out to all sides, poking out over the couch and toward the front door (see my photo insert). This was obviously dangerous, so my mom hung Kleenex tissues on the tips of all the branches. It's a look I've yet to see in *Better Homes and Gardens*. It's a miracle no one lost an eye.

But my parents will still tell you it was worth it to watch a very grainy image of their daughter anchoring the news on TV. My mom started to brag that she was "Patti Ann Browne's mother." It was incredibly gratifying to know that my parents were proud of me and that their sacrifices were starting to reap rewards. Their belief in me never wavered.

It was a modest beginning, but I was on my way.

TV 55's news department at that time consisted of two people: myself and Steve Hutnikoff. I was the news director, assignment editor, producer, field reporter, copywriter, and anchor. Steve was the videographer, editor, and studio camera operator. Thankfully, I already had experience as a news director from my Fordham days. Also thankfully, I got along well with Steve!

But within a short time, I was outgrowing this job. I had my eyes on News 12 Long Island, a local 24-hour cable news network. But that outfit only hired people who had worked for a network affiliate. The New York market—the biggest in the country—was out of reach at that stage. It looked like I would have to move to a mid-sized TV market to cut my teeth before moving back.

Leaving my family and friends to live someplace where I didn't know a soul wasn't something I wanted to do. But since broadcast news was my chosen career, it seemed inevitable. So, I found a list of television markets in size order. I focused on the markets in the middle. One caught my eye immediately. Right there in my target zone was South Bend, Indiana. As it happened, my twin sister was there, attending Notre Dame Law School.

I had visited Colleen several times, and I loved the environment. I even drove out with my high school gang in a Winnebago for a "Fighting Irish" football weekend. We had a blast.

Wouldn't it be great if I could get a job working in South Bend, and hang out with my sister and her law school pals and go to games on weekends?

Unfortunately, there were no published openings at any of the three network affiliates in South Bend. Undeterred, I sent my resume and a tape of my on-air work to the ABC, NBC, and CBS stations there.

To my surprise, I got a call from what was then the ABC affiliate, WSJV. Since South Bend is near Indiana's border with Michigan, they were starting up a Michigan Bureau and needed a bureau chief who would gather news out in the field and then anchor a Michigan segment on their nightly newscast.

They flew me out for an interview, and I got the job!

In the years prior, I had heard a lot of talk about how getting a job in broadcast news was all about "who you know." But it can also be about *what* you know. I had no connections. I was just a middle-class girl from Queens who learned my trade by starting at the bottom.

So when people ask me for career advice, I recommend that they not stress out too much about "networking." I know that works for some people. But if you're an introvert like me, you can still get ahead by distinguishing yourself through your work. And when opportunities arise, you will have the skills to take them.

My parents and grandparents were right. America was a "land of opportunity," where hard work eventually paid off. Thanks to my diligence, my parents' support, and God's blessings, I was off to the Midwest.

CHAPTER 5

Plant Another Crop, See What Grows

I arrived in South Bend, Indiana, during one of the coldest and snowiest winters on record there. And that's saying a lot, because South Bend is in the shadow of Lake Michigan, where the "lake effect" meant *every* winter there was cold and snowy.

It seemed like each morning, I had to allow an extra 15 minutes to dig out my car from under the foot of snow that had fallen overnight. My days of not knowing how to drive in snow were soon a distant memory. The commute from South Bend up to my bureau in lower Michigan was often treacherous—the road surface alternating between slippery slush and a sheet of ice. It was just a 20-minute drive in dry conditions, but it was almost never dry.

I quickly discovered that my New York wardrobe needed winterizing. The high heels I was planning to wear to conduct interviews were chucked in the back of my closet, replaced by heavy-duty snow boots. Instead of blouses, I stocked up on turtlenecks in every color. I didn't bother styling my hair in the morning. It was only going to get flattened under a hat.

Having lived my entire life in New York City, South Bend seemed small to me. And I wasn't even working in South Bend itself, which was actually a bustling college town. My daily "beat," Berrien and Cass counties in Michigan, was even smaller.

And the pace of life was slow. Even the pace at which people *spoke* seemed slow to me. An impatient New Yorker who was accustomed to doing everything fast, I was frequently exasperated by rural Midwesterners' lack of a sense of urgency. They also didn't get my sarcastic sense of humor. They thought I was being rude at times when I was trying to be funny.

I was starting to wonder what I had gotten myself into. I had to keep reminding myself that my contract was only for a year. I told myself: Just do the year, get your experience, and then get out of here and back to New York. I must admit that for the first few months, I narrow-mindedly viewed South Bend as a pit stop on my road to bigger and better things. How wrong I was.

The ABC station for the South Bend market was located in Elkhart, Indiana, but my Michigan bureau was at the Four Flags Hotel in Niles. So unless I was filling in as main anchor, I wasn't around most of the WSJV gang.

After a few weeks of training, my days were spent solely with my bureau's videographer, Don Schoenfeld. He and I drove around rural Michigan shooting interviews and video. Then I would write a script and he'd edit the video, and we would broadcast my live nightly segment from a quaint little anchor set on the hotel's ground floor.

Soon after I arrived in town, WSJV started running a teaser campaign to promote Newswatch 28's new Michigan Bureau. Roadside billboards featured my photo with a caption that simply read: *Do you know this woman?*

This was quite puzzling to Colleen's Notre Dame classmates—many of whom didn't know she had a twin sister. They started asking her, "Colleen, why are there billboards with your picture asking who you are?"

They soon got their answer. First of all, they started seeing me on TV. Secondly, "follow-up" billboards explained who I was. Thirdly, Colleen took me with her to some campus events and introduced me around.

Two of my cousins, Patti and Mikki, were also at Notre Dame. It was a fun group. Since everyone was already settled in dorms, I was renting a two-bedroom apartment off-campus with an undergrad named Tina. Colleen was buried in her law books and I was working, so we didn't hang out as much as I had anticipated. But I joined her, her friends, and our cousins on some fun nights out downtown. And I attended weekly Mass in the law school chapel, which was great because the sermons were directed at people our age.

At some point, my parents flew out to visit Colleen and me. They asked if I would mind if they sat in my studio during my live broadcast.

My dad emphasized, "Only if you're comfortable.... We don't want to be a distraction."

I scoffed, "Dad, I've done this hundreds of times. It's fine!"

I had been nervous during my first few Michigan segments, as I always was when starting a new job. But it quickly became old hat. I was live five nights a week. I didn't even think about it. Stage fright was simply not an issue for me.

So when my videographer Don and I got back to the bureau, I wrote my scripts, and he edited my video as usual. I fixed my hair and makeup. I taped my scripts together and loaded them on the prompter, which I would control with a remote in my hand.

Then my parents and sister arrived, and I gave them seats in the corner. I sat in my anchor chair and put on my microphone. ABC's *World News Tonight* was wrapping up on the monitor. (In that market, the network news ran before the local news.)

My dad started going on excitedly about how incredible it was.

"Just think…. Right now, we're watching Peter Jennings, along with millions of other people. But in just a few minutes, hundreds of thousands of people will be watching Patti Ann, right here in this studio! This very room will be live…on air…to hundreds of thousands of people!"

I felt a lump starting to rise up in my throat.

Jennings was done, we were in commercial, and then WSJV's main anchors, Michelle Gary and Mike Nikitas, were on screen. I had the top story. They started to toss to me.

"Stand by!" Don said, as he had every day for months. Why did it sound so scary this time?

The lump was huge now—like an apple stuck in my throat. I was on a split-screen with the main set, and the anchors were saying, "Patti Ann Browne has that story live from our Michigan Bureau. Patti Ann?"

I could barely breathe, never mind speak. I swallowed hard, trying to push the lump down. I choked out the first few words on the prompter. Couldn't breathe…. Paused to swallow again, mid-sentence…sputtered out a few more words. My eyes were staring into the camera, unblinking. I swallowed again…a few more words.

In the corner of my eye, I saw my mom drop her head down between her knees and cover her ears with her hands. You know, like when a plane is crashing.

A few more words, a few more gulps, and at last, I got to a sound bite. I was able to stop talking for a few seconds. I tried to breathe.

The director in the control room in Elkhart asked Don in his headset, "What's wrong with her?"

I didn't hear that, but I could hear Don's mumbled response: "*Her parents are here.*"

As the sound bite played out, no one else said a word. What was there to say?

Then I was back on, a little better now. The lump was maybe a plum instead of an apple. I got through it, but it was bad. Really bad. I wondered if I would be fired.

Once I tossed back to the main set, my parents jumped up and said, "We're so sorry! We never should have come here."

"It's not your fault," I assured them. "I thought it would be fine! I don't know what happened. Mom, why did you put your head between your knees?"

She explained that it was obvious that she and my dad were the problem, so she wanted to signal to me that they were "gone." They couldn't actually walk out of the studio. (That would look bad.) So she figured she would cover her ears and shield her eyes as a way of letting me know she was not watching or listening. To me, it came across more like she was in the throes of deep despair over having such a failure for a daughter, but I appreciated her trying.

I got a call from my news director after the show. I explained that I somehow got stage fright because my parents were there. Fortunately for me, Larry Ford was a super nice guy. He said he understood, but I was never to allow spectators in the studio again.

"Yes. Of course. Never. Ever!"

He told me, "You're doing a fine job."

And that was it. It took me a long time to get over that incident, but I was thankful to have an understanding boss who recognized that I was only human. Needless to say, my parents have never asked to watch me do a live broadcast again.

Soon enough, I was dating Don the videographer. Like me, he was a young single from a big city (Chicago) who took the job in South Bend as a résumé builder. It was like a Hallmark movie plot: "*Two city slickers end up stuck with each other in a tiny Michigan town, grappling with snow storms, culture shock...and romance.*"

Don was a wonderful guy, and together he and I learned to appreciate small-town life. We covered tractor pulls, county fairs, and swine shows. Don and I heard crop reports and tornado warnings on the radio. We covered dune erosion at Lake Michigan, hunting stories, and the devastating job losses resulting from the closures of area automotive plants.

Our coverage area was mainly farms and livestock. Berrien County was home to a "fruit belt," where peaches, apples, pears, berries, and other fruits grew abundantly.

Cass County was big into hogs. One day, we went to interview a mayor—not at "city hall," of course. We knocked on the door of his farmhouse, and his wife told us he was "out back, immunizing cattle." We had to wade through a pen full of adorable pigs to get to the mayor in a field behind them. I gleefully commented to Don that these pigs were just the cutest things, with their little pink snouts and curly tails.

When our interview concluded, we were headed back to our news vehicle when the mayor called after us.

"Wait! I have something for you."

Back in New York, interviewees never felt compelled to give the news crews anything. (And if a reporter is given something too valuable, it could be considered a bribe.) But Midwestern hospitality dictated that if someone came to your home, you obviously offered them food or drink.

Catching up to us, the mayor proudly handed over a package wrapped in paper. It was sausage.

He beamed, "We just slaughtered the pig yesterday!"

I had no right to be horrified. I'm not a vegetarian. But we city folk get our meat from a supermarket, and we don't think about how it got there. It was a rude awakening.

The sausage was really tasty, by the way.

At some point, in the dead of winter, we were blessed by a few days of unseasonably warm weather. At least, to me it seemed like a blessing.

I called my news director at the main station, as I did every morning from the bureau, to go over possible story ideas for that night's Michigan segment. I had a few topics in mind, but Larry dismissed them all.

"Obviously you have to cover the peaches."

I had no idea what he was talking about.

"The peaches!" he repeated. "The weather! The peach crop is in danger."

What? The weather was beautiful. I still wasn't getting it, so Larry patiently explained.

"If the weather gets too warm in the winter, the peach trees think spring is arriving, and the sap starts to rise up the trunks. Then when it gets cold again, the sap freezes and expands, splitting open the tree trunks, killing the whole crop."

"That's terrible!" I replied.

I booked an interview with a peach farmer in Berrien County, and Don and I drove to his farm. We had passed it many times while driving to other stories, but I had never really looked at it. Rows of peach trees stretched as far as the eye could see in either direction. Standing in their midst was a farmer in overalls, hands on his hips, shaking his head with a deeply furrowed brow.

He and I strolled through the orchard while I asked stupid questions like, "Can't you put air conditioners out here to keep the trees cold?"

It was too late for that (not that it would've worked anyway). He cut into a trunk with a knife, pressed his hand into the cut, and showed me the sap on his finger. The sap had already risen.

Still convinced there was a solution, I pressed on. "So when it gets cold again, can you put heaters out here to prevent the trees from re-freezing?"

The farmer kindly pointed out that he had acres and acres of peach trees, and none of them were near electrical outlets. He said it was basically inevitable that his entire crop would be lost.

We ran the story that night, but I stubbornly refused to believe that the trees would actually die. We moved on to other stories, and within days the cold returned.

A few days later, Don was driving us along that familiar road which led to most of our interviews when I glanced over at the peach farm.

"The peach trees!" I exclaimed.

It was a devastating sight. Every single tree, row after row, was split right down the middle of the trunk—their dark, leafless branches resting in the snow on either side. I felt tears well up in my eyes.

I asked Don to pull over. Since we had covered this story, we needed to run a follow-up.

I found the farmer and asked him, "What will you do?"

The old man shrugged and said, "Wait till next year, plant another crop, be patient, see what grows."

I stared at him.

This farmer had just lost an entire year's worth of work and income. But he didn't seem angry. He had the patience to "wait till next year," the optimism to "plant another crop," and the acceptance of nature's unpredictability to "see what grows."

How could he possibly be so calm? I was a control freak. I could not tolerate that level of uncertainty. In that moment, I finally began to understand the people I had been covering for the past few months. I had a new respect and admiration for the farmer's way of life and philosophy.

I had gone there to learn about reporting for an affiliate. But God sent me there to learn other lessons too. Slow down, look around, be patient, accept what you can't change, stay calm, keep trying. It was the Midwest way. (That, and always have fresh muffins ready for guests.)

Don's hometown in Chicago was just an hour and a half away from South Bend, so we spent many weekends in the Windy City. We hung out with his family, rode bikes on a trail along Lake Michigan, went to Cubs games, and attended barbecues and weddings with Don's friends. I loved Chicago. I could not believe there were beaches right there—walking distance from the skyscrapers! True, it was a lake, not an ocean, but Lake Michigan is enormous, and its beaches are large and sandy.

We even went up to Milwaukee, Wisconsin, for Summer Fest. What an event! Hundreds of bands performed on multiple outdoor stages on the shores of Lake Michigan over the course of several weekends. Crowds stood around in T-shirts and shorts, drinking beer from plastic cups and dancing to the music.

Summer back in southwest Michigan was also glorious. A far cry from the seemingly endless bleak, gray winter, summer bathed the rolling hills in bright sunshine and rich color. The cows grazed on green grass under a clear blue sky, and classic red barns dotted the landscape. Roadside farm stands sold fresh produce and pies. The Benton Harbor Lighthouse stood as a picturesque landmark in Lake Michigan.

In the winter, I always hoped the news would break nearby so we wouldn't have to travel far in the snow and ice. But now in summer, I looked forward to lengthy drives along winding country roads full of rustic scenery.

When fall rolled around, Colleen was starting a new semester, so she was free to move into my apartment with me. It was great living with her again. We borrowed each other's suits, and I attended Fighting Irish football games with Colleen and her friends. I prayed at the beautiful grotto on campus and jogged around St. Mary's Lake. I felt like a law student (except for the whole studying law part).

Despite its inauspicious start, my year in the Midwest turned out to be wonderful. I arrived thinking I would tolerate living there for a year as a stepping stone. But I ended up falling in love with the area and with Don. When my contract ended, I was offered a new deal lasting three years. Seeing how happy I was, my WSJV bosses expected me to take it.

But I was at a crossroads. I wanted to go home. Colleen and my cousins would be graduating and leaving, along with all my new temporary friends from Notre Dame. I still had Don and all of his friends and relatives. But I missed my own family and friends.

I was torn. So I figured I'd leave it to fate. I sent a tape and resume to News 12 Long Island. If I got a job there, I'd consider it a sign that I was meant to leave. If I didn't, that meant I should stay in South Bend.

I got the job at News 12. I packed up my belongings with a heavy heart and cried my eyes out when I walked out of my apartment for the last time.

Don and I tried to make it work long distance, but it didn't last. Don never went back to Chicago. He was in love with South Bend, too, and eventually with a wonderful woman who lived there. They are happily married with kids. It all worked out the way it was supposed to.

When young people from New York ask me for career advice, they always want to know, "Do I really have to move somewhere else to get experience?"

I urge them to embrace the opportunity to expand their horizons. I have wonderful memories of my year in South Bend, and the Midwest will always hold a special place in my heart.

CHAPTER 6

Jumping the Fence

The water was rising fast around our news vehicle. The car had no power, the windows and doors wouldn't open, and it suddenly occurred to me that I could actually die.

Things had seemed fine just minutes earlier. News 12 had sent me out along with my videographer, Steve, to cover flooding in Freeport in the wake of one of Long Island's infamous nor'easter storms.

The storm had passed and the weather was calm, but the flooding hadn't happened yet. A storm surge often occurs after the rains end, and we knew from experience that it was coming. We drove out to the end of a long peninsula between two canals, known as the Nautical Mile, where over-washes were common. The boats docked in the water were getting higher and higher. I thought how strange it was to be looking *up* at a boat in the water, instead of down.

Wanting a good backdrop, we met up with a firefighter at the edge of the pier to get some on-camera comments about flood preparations. The interview over, Steve asked the firefighter approximately how much time we had left to shoot video before we needed to "get out of Dodge."

He told us we had about 15 minutes. Then he drove off. Steve started shooting some B-roll with me by his side.

Less than five minutes later, we heard an unsettling slushy sound. Looking to our right, we saw water spilling out over the pier, under boats that towered over us menacingly. A loud rumbling sound soon accompanied the sound of rushing water. Steve yelled, "Run!"

You didn't have to tell me twice.

With sea water swirling under our feet, we sprinted to our news car—Steve lugging a heavy camera and audio box, I in my cute but impractical high heels. It was a short distance to the car, but by the time we got there, the water was halfway up the tires.

We jumped in and Steve quickly got the car in gear. We started driving down the pier, the water so high around our car that it was throwing a wake. It felt almost like we were in a boat, but sadly that was not the case.

The car was moving very slowly through the deep water, and when we were about halfway down the pier, it stopped running. The tires were now completely submerged, and the water was halfway up the car doors.

This seemed like a good time to get out. We pushed against our doors but the water was too heavy around them. We tried to roll down our windows so we could climb out, but they were power windows and we had no power. Steve grabbed the bulky mobile phone off of its base under the dashboard. But back then the phones were connected to the car battery. He tried anyway. There was no dial tone. We were trapped.

I berated myself for never having learned what to do in this scenario. Too late now. This might be how I died. I said a silent prayer.

As Steve and I pondered our fate, we saw a firetruck heading up the pier toward us. It was the guy we had just interviewed. He had figured out that his estimate was off and thought he should check on us.

As he drove his enormous firetruck past us, he signaled to Steve to put his car in gear. Then he turned his truck around, positioned it behind our car, and pushed our car out of the flood with his truck. A minute or two later, we were safe and sound.

We thanked the firefighter profusely for saving our lives. But I was haunted by the question: *What if he hadn't come back for us?* There was no one else around. No one would've heard our screams from inside the car. Although it was quickly resolved, this was a close call. I was grateful to be alive.

I know now that if you're trapped in a car in a flood and can't get out, you should try to break the windows before the water gets to them (after that, it's not safe). Use a glass breaker if you keep one in your car, or try a capped pen or anything with a hard pointy edge that you can thrust with force against the glass to make it shatter. If your seat's headrest pulls out, you can slam the two steel pegs against the window to smash it.

If you can't break a window, hold your breath and let the car fill with water. Once the car is full, the pressure will be equalized, allowing you to open the doors and swim out. While you're waiting, remove your seat belt, turn on your lights and unlock your doors. If emergency personnel are nearby, they can spot you more easily with your lights on, and they can open the doors if they're unlocked. You should also remove extra layers of clothing in case you need to swim to the surface.

Ideally, don't drive anywhere near a flooded area. If you encounter a large puddle in the middle of the road, assume it could get even larger, and back up. While you're backing up, roll down your windows, just in case.

That concludes this public service announcement.

Being trapped in a car in a flood was one of the more dramatic adventures I had while reporting for News 12. But there were others, such as getting trapped in the United Nations building in Manhattan.

I was there to cover a big UN Security Council vote. When the story is so big that too many cameras would be fighting for space, the media use a "pool." One camera person is assigned to shoot the proceedings, and copies of their footage are made available to all the other press in attendance.

So while the pool crew shot this debate and vote, the reporters sat in a room set aside for media, listening to a feed of the speeches, writing our stories, and chatting with each other. Once the vote had taken place, we were escorted through winding hallways and down staircases to a tiny room somewhere in the basement. A man there was in charge of making dubs for all of us.

The vote occurred late in the day, and all of us needed this story for the top of our newscasts. The dubbing process back then was painfully slow. The correspondents for the big networks got first dibs so that they could air the footage on their national news programs. Then the reporters for the network affiliates got their copies. Representing News 12, a cable channel that still didn't get the respect it deserved, I was dead last.

By the time he handed me my tape, at least an hour had elapsed. I had very little time to get that video to our live truck outside the building, scroll through to find a key sound bite, have it edited, and jump in front of a camera for my live shot. Knowing how tight the timing was, I bolted out of that little room and sprinted to a staircase. I ran up a flight, then another, then paused. *Was it one flight or two? Am I even on the right staircase?* I realized I had not paid close enough attention when I was being led down to that room. I exited the stairwell and looked up and down the hallway. It didn't look familiar. And it was completely empty.

I ran back down a flight, then checked that hallway. Also deserted. *Don't panic*, I told myself. *Just walk down this hallway and look for EXIT signs, or a person.* Walking the length of the hall, I found neither. I turned back and walked through several side hallways. I think at some point I spotted an emergency exit, but it would trigger an alarm and it seemed to lead to the wrong side of the building, so I wandered on.

It was remarkable how quickly everyone had cleared out of this building! It had been teeming with people just an hour or two earlier. Now it was so quiet, I could hear my rapid footsteps echoing off the walls. I was alone in this vast, empty complex. And I was lost. Anyone who's been in that building can attest to the fact that it's a maze.

No problem; I'll just retrace my steps back to the man in the basement. But where was he again? I ran around breathlessly until I finally found the little room. The door was locked. I knocked. No one answered. Of course he was long gone. I'm sure he cleared out the second he finished my dub. Must be easy to leave when you know the way out!

I have no idea how long I wandered the vacant halls of the UN before I finally found an exit. As I stepped out of the building, eerie quiet was instantly replaced by noisy chaos. Reporters and satellite trucks were lined up along the sidewalk, about to go live with the story. There was just one problem. They were all on the outside of a fence. I was on the inside. I ran to a gate. It was locked. *You must be kidding me.*

My live truck operator spotted me and started yelling, "Patti Ann! You're on in less than five!" He pointed to his watch to make the point.

I yelled back, "How do I get out of here?!"

That caught all the reporters' attention. Local CBS reporter Mark Schumacher, whom I knew from the Long Island beat, spun around, mic in hand, and asked me, "Patti Ann, are you *trapped*?"

"Apparently, yes!"

All the reporters were now staring at me, marveling at my predicament.

"Patti Ann!! Three minutes!" It was my truck op again, leaning out the truck door, holding the mobile phone to his ear, where he was obviously getting chewed out by the control room.

One reporter suggested we shoot the live shot through the bars. No, not enough time to set up. Calmly assessing the situation, Mark said, "You'll have to jump the fence."

Jump the fence? Of the United Nations building? That must be some kind of felony. But is it really a crime if I'm climbing *out* of the building instead of *in*?

"Patti Ann, two minutes!!!"

Oh, what the heck. The fence wasn't terribly high. I threw my stuff over it and grabbed the bars. As I recall, Mark's videographer, Mike Muskopf, pushed an equipment box against the fence, which I was able to stand on through the bars. Somehow or another, I got to the other side. (Turns out there was an open gate in the opposite direction from the one I checked, which would've been helpful to know earlier.) Anyway, I had no time to think about it.

My cameraman handed me a mic, shoved an earpiece in my ear, and within seconds the anchor in the studio was saying, "Patti Ann Browne is live right now at the United Nations with more. Patti Ann?"

I had no sound bite but I had written a full script on my pad while waiting, so I was able to deliver the story just fine. (Even if I hadn't gotten lost, I doubt I would've had time to cut sound before my hit, given how late I got the dub.) We turned the sound around for the next live hit. The process is quicker now in the digital age. But being a reporter isn't what I'd call a relaxing job.

People used to frequently ask me, "Who writes your stories?" They seemed to think some poor nameless grunts were busting their butts doing all the work, so that I could simply breeze in front of the camera and take credit for their efforts. That was not the case during any of my earlier jobs. I did almost everything myself.

At News 12, an assignment editor would give me a story topic or maybe an article from that morning's *Newsday*. On a very good day, the desk might have booked my first interview for me. But more often, I would decide who to interview, look up their numbers in the phone book (no internet yet), and schedule the interviews. I'd figure out directions from a Hagstrom map (no smart phones) and navigate for my videographer, who was driving. I would come up with questions in the car and then ask those questions with the camera rolling, as well as follow-ups that came to mind during the interview. We'd shoot some B-roll, then hop back in the car and repeat the process for my second and maybe third interviews.

By then, I hopefully had an idea of how the finished story would look, so I'd jot down an on-camera "standup," memorize it, and we'd shoot it at a relevant location. On the drive back to the studio, I would play through my interviews on a mini tape recorder I held along with my mic. I'd choose my sound bites and hand-write my script in the car.

Once back at the station, I'd log the video shot by my videographer and tweak my script to make sure it matched the pictures. Then I'd give my handwritten script to a copy editor for approval, or if I had a few extra minutes I'd type it up. Then I'd voice my tracks in the audio booth, and sit with an editor to put it all together as a "package."

If I were live from the scene, it was a similar process except those last parts were done in a cramped truck. I had less than eight hours to do all of the above—and half that time when assigned two stories in one day, which happened often. And I did this five days a week.

Over the weekend, I might bump into an acquaintance who had seen me on TV, and they'd ask who writes my stories....

"I write my own stories!"

But many people don't realize that. On one occasion, a friend of a friend asked me for advice regarding how her daughter could become a reporter. I asked if the daughter was majoring in communications or political science at her college. No, fashion.

"Is she involved in her college radio or TV station?"

"No."

"Does she have an internship anywhere?"

"Yes, with a designer."

I noted that this wouldn't be all that useful for an aspiring journalist. The mom replied, "But she's beautiful, so I'm sure she can get a job like yours without a problem."

I gave it one more shot: "Does she write for the school newspaper?"

The mom responded impatiently, "She doesn't want to write news. She wants to do what *you* do!"

I had to explain that I write news. This type of conversation took place many times throughout my career.

And I had it easy. Now, thanks to digital cameras and tablets, most reporters at smaller stations are required to shoot and even edit their own stuff, in addition to everything described above. It's still worth it if you love it, as I did. But you have to love it.

Even when they're not scrambling to meet an impossible deadline or risking their lives to cover a storm, reporters experience emotional stress almost every day. News is usually bad, and covering it can be depressing.

I was one of the first on the scene after the Long Island Railroad massacre in 1993. Twenty-five people were shot on a commuter train heading home from Manhattan. Six died. When Steve and I arrived at the Merillon Avenue station in Garden City, I was completely unprepared for what I was seeing. It was horrible. I was live all night from the scene. I don't want to relive it. Colin Ferguson was later convicted and remains imprisoned at Attica. I still show up in documentaries about this tragedy.

I also covered the aftermath of the 1993 World Trade Center bombing. Little did I know it would be a precursor to an even worse terrorist attack eight years later.

I covered many homicides as well. Interviewing neighbors after a couple was murdered in their home, I spotted a dog wandering around the property. A neighbor said it was the couple's dog. It now had no family. Sometimes it's a small detail that hits the hardest.

I also covered politics. I reported live from George Pataki's campaign headquarters the night he was elected governor of New

York State. I went live from Albany covering state Supreme Court cases, and live from Washington, DC, when a Long Island story became a national one.

There were lighter moments as well. I had a boa constrictor wrapped around me for a standup for a "kicker" story to air at the end of a newscast. I've always liked snakes, and the handler assured me the boa was friendly. Boa constrictors are non-venomous, but they can squeeze a small person to death if agitated. Luckily, I didn't agitate this one.

After a while, News 12 promoted me from full-time reporter to weekend anchor with Joe Moskowitz. He's a terrific guy, and we had fun with sportscaster Mike Zimet and meteorologist Norm Dvoskin. In addition to anchoring the 5 and 10 PM newscasts on Saturdays and Sundays, I reported three weekdays, also on the late shift. And I filled in as weekday anchor, sharing the desk now and then with Lea Tyrrell, Scott Feldman, Doug Geed, and Judy Martin.

Judy was one of a kind—funny, outspoken, and caring. We continued to get together long after I left News 12. She was taken from us way too soon, passing away suddenly at age 49 after complaining to friends about side effects from a blood thinner after knee surgery. I still miss her.

Since my hours at News 12 were late, I was free in the mornings to fill in occasionally as morning-drive news anchor on Long Island's popular rock radio station WBAB-FM. I only did this a handful of times when Tracy Burgess was off, but it was fun to be back in a radio studio and a thrill to be on-air with Hall of Fame DJ Bob Buchmann.

But working weekends and nights made it almost impossible to have a life outside of the newsroom. I missed barbecues, weddings, and ball games. The extent of my social life was grabbing a beer with News 12's *Night Edition* crew after our late newscast ended at 11 PM.

My hours were crazy during my entire time at News 12, so I guess it was inevitable that my boyfriends were co-workers. I had two serious relationships during my years at News 12. Both were with talented videographers. I was frequently paired with them on stories, which gave us lots of time to chat in the car. Eventually, romances developed.

There were advantages to dating co-workers, like having the same friends and understanding when the other person complained about work. Also, we made great teams out in the field and produced some top quality work.

But it got complicated when we broke up. I ended both relationships amicably, but my heart was still hurting. It's difficult to see your ex-boyfriend every day when you're trying to get over him. We were all professionals and we did our jobs, regardless. But there were some uncomfortable car rides.

From that time on, all my serious boyfriends were men who had no connection to the news industry. And I vowed to keep my social life separate from my job.

A few years into my time at News 12, I was named full-time co-anchor of the three-hour morning show with Carol Silva. It was the channel's highest rated program. Long Islanders made a habit of watching while getting ready for work, mainly for the local weather and traffic.

Anchoring full-time is very different from reporting. As a reporter, I was "out in the field" for most of the day. Anchors rarely leave the station. They're at their desks preparing for the show.

At News 12, I had to write one or two blocks of our newscast and copyedit everything else I was reading. It's less exciting but also less stressful.

I woke up each morning at 3 AM to get to the station at 4 AM, to prepare to be live from 6 to 9 AM. I greatly enjoyed my years anchoring with Carol and our meteorologist, Joe Cioffi. Carol was like a big sister who gave great advice. Joe liked to clown around off-camera, and we had lots of laughs during commercial breaks, along with the crew.

My parents caught part of my morning show one day while they were visiting the Hamptons. I was doing a cooking segment. My guest was extolling the virtues of horseradish, saying it's not just for the Jewish holidays. In fact, he said, it's delicious for breakfast when added to tomato juice. I know some people like horseradish in their Bloody Mary, but I've never been a fan of either horseradish or tomato juice, especially at 7 in the morning. Yet it was understood that I would try this concoction when he offered it to me live on air.

My parents were saying to each other, "She's not really going to drink that, is she? This could be ugly."

The camera zoomed in for a close-up as I took a sip. I tried to brace myself, but when I swallowed it, my entire body shuddered involuntarily, my eyes crossed, and my mouth contorted as I struggled not to spit it out or vomit.

I got my game face back in a second or two, as my guest waited for my verdict. I wasn't going to lie and say it was delicious, so I simply smiled through watery eyes and said, "Interesting!"

My parents say they were laughing so hard they were in tears.

They didn't tell me they had seen the segment, but when exchanging presents that Christmas, they handed me a small, wrapped, extra gift. I opened it and found a bottle of horseradish.

We interviewed many celebrities on the morning show—some in person, others by satellite. Either way, I thought it was pretty exciting. In my early career, I interviewed Mark Hamill, Roger Daltrey, Kiefer Sutherland, James Patterson, Jerry Orbach, Jeff Foxworthy, and many others. I also dated a couple of Jets players (during two different football seasons, of course). And I met politicians in every tier of government.

Meanwhile, I was a very minor "celebrity" in my own right on Long Island. Just as a sample, according to an old schedule I dug up, over a three-month period I judged a Trivia Challenge for United Cerebral Palsy, emceed a Boy Scout dinner, spoke at a New York State Women's Political Caucus event, emceed a Teen Community Awards ceremony, spoke to fifth graders at a middle school, and made a guest appearance at a leukemia fundraiser. Interacting with the community is one of the pleasures of working in local news.

I also hosted parts of the telethon for The Prayer Channel of the Brooklyn Diocese every year for many years.

But my newfound fame came with a cost. I had my first stalker when I was at News 12. He was a cop. I was driving home from work one day when he pulled up behind me on the Long Island Expressway, lights flashing and sirens blaring. For the life of me, I couldn't figure out what I had done wrong. I pulled onto the shoulder and stopped. He came to my window and said, "You're Patti Ann Browne, right?"

"Yes," I said, momentarily pleased that perhaps my "fame" might help me get out of whatever unknown trouble I was in.

"I knew it was you!" he said. "I watch you every morning while I work out. I'm an NYPD lieutenant. Where are you headed?"

"I'm headed home," I replied, suddenly feeling uneasy and not wanting to tell him where I lived. "Officer, may I ask, what did I do wrong?"

"What?" he looked confused. "Oh, nothing! I just wanted to meet you! So where do you live?"

The hairs were standing up on the back of my neck, so I gestured in the direction I was heading and said vaguely, "Oh, over there."

Undeterred, he told me his name. We'll call him Lieutenant Smith. He asked if I had a boyfriend.

I said yes, and that I was in a hurry....

He leaned against my open window and continued to chat about how he watched Carol Silva and me every morning. I got a really bad feeling in my gut.

Finally, he stood up and said goodbye. My heart was racing as I pulled back onto the road.

Unfortunately, my exit in Queens was just ahead. I exited off the highway and made my usual turn. I checked my rearview mirror.

Shit, he's following me!

I absolutely did not want this guy to know where I lived, so I drove to the local drug store to lose him. He followed me into the parking lot. I got out of my car, and he jumped out of his and raced me to the door, blocking me from entering the store.

"So you live in my precinct! You should call me some time," he said insistently.

"I'm sorry but I have a boyfriend," I said again, as I had in the car. He continued to block my path while trying to chat more. Finally, I said, "I'm really in a hurry," and circled around him with trepidation. He eventually let me pass and I was thankful that he didn't follow me inside.

But I wandered around the store for a very long time, roaming the aisles, my heart beating out of my chest. I probably looked like a shoplifter.

Finally, I bought something and left. I was thankful to not see a police car in the lot.

I drove to my apartment complex, where I lived alone. I parked on the street and went inside, carefully locking the door. I called my boyfriend and told him what had happened. He couldn't figure out why I was so upset.

"This doesn't sound like that big a deal," he said.

"I'm telling you: this isn't over!" I insisted. I could feel it.

The next day when I left for work, the lieutenant's business card was tucked into my windshield wiper with a note: "Call me."

I'm so stupid! I thought. *Obviously a cop can find out my address. He probably ran my plate.* Totally against the rules, but so is pulling over a woman so you can ask her out. This guy clearly didn't care. And now he knew where I lived.

Thankfully, it was Friday, and I headed to my share house for the weekend. When I returned Sunday evening, I parked and went into my apartment, and within a minute my buzzer went off.

Without thinking, I pressed the button and asked, "Who is it?"

"Patti Ann, it's Lieutenant Smith. Can I come in?"

My heart was in my mouth. I hadn't seen his car. Had he hidden it? And what was he doing here? Had he waited for me all day? All *weekend*?

"Sorry, I'm busy," I said.

He buzzed again. I didn't answer. I just stared at the box on the wall, frozen. I waited a minute, then stared out the window of my ground-floor apartment. I didn't see him walk away. Was he still outside my door?

I knew this was going to be a problem!

I called my sister Mary Lou, who lived across the street in the same complex, and told her what had happened. Her husband, Jim, overheard parts of the conversation and came on the phone and said, "There's been a cop car sitting on our corner all weekend. I saw it every time I walked the dog. I thought someone was under surveillance."

My God, he had spent the entire weekend staking out my apartment complex, waiting for me to come home! What should I do? Mary Lou and Jim were concerned but said we could only hope maybe he would give up, since I had blown him off. My boyfriend had the same advice. But I already knew from my three brief encounters with him that this guy was not the type to give up.

I didn't sleep at all that night. The next morning, I left my apartment before dawn, as usual, for my News 12 morning show. I was on edge as I stepped out of my building into the quiet darkness. I frantically looked left and right as I sprinted to my car parked around the corner. I was panting as I fumbled with my key in the car lock. Safe in my vehicle, I started driving, praying again that I would not see an NYPD car.

My drive to work was uneventful, as was my drive home that afternoon, until I entered my hallway.

My neighbor opened his door and said, "Hey, there was a cop here looking for you before."

"What?!" I said. "What did he say?"

"He was waiting outside the building door so I let him in, and he started reading all the mailboxes. I was about to go into my apartment, but he stopped me and asked, 'Which apartment is Patti Ann Browne's?'"

"You didn't tell him, did you?" I asked, in a very panicked voice. It hadn't occurred to me that my neighbor was thinking I must be under investigation for something.

"Of course I told him. He's a cop."

"No!" I yelled. "He's the bad guy! He's stalking me."

My neighbor looked confused, like he wasn't sure who to believe, and yet he wasn't completely surprised. After a few seconds, he said, "Honestly, I thought his questions were a little weird. He asked me where you go during the day and what you do. I said after you come home, you usually go out for a run, and his eyes got really excited and he said, 'She runs?! Where? When?' He was very insistent, kind of crazy, so I told him I had no idea where you run."

I could see that my neighbor fully grasped the situation now.

In a calmer voice, I asked him to please never answer any more questions if this cop came around again.

"Patti Ann," he said. "He's a cop. I can't *not* answer his questions. It's a tough situation."

"I understand. You have to do what you have to do. But please believe me when I tell you he has no business being here, and he has no legitimate reason for asking questions about me. He's a stalker. He's abusing his power."

"You should report him," he said.

"To whom?" I asked. "He's a lieutenant *in our precinct*. Calling the cops is probably not the best move."

"Good point," he shrugged and went into his apartment.

My boyfriend still said there was nothing to worry about. "He's weird and annoying, but it's not like he's going to hurt you. He's in love with you."

"He's not in love!" I countered. "He's obsessed. There's a difference. Obsessed people eventually crack when the object of their obsession rebuffs them. At that point they *do* turn dangerous."

I had been in the news business long enough to have reported on this type of scenario.

About a week later, I was running on my favorite path along the water, next to a highway. A police car drove slowly past me. There was a young officer looking at me sheepishly, and next to him was Lieutenant Smith. I turned and ran in the opposite direction, knowing it would be impossible for the car to turn around on the path.

Dammit. Someone had obviously told him where I ran.

Returning to my apartment, the neighbor with whom I'd spoken before came out again, as did the woman in the unit next to his.

"We have to talk," they said.

Both of them said Lieutenant Smith had been harassing them, hanging around outside the building, stopping any neighbors who entered, and interrogating them about me.

The guy said, "And he's not so cheerful anymore. He's very angry. He's ranting about how you used to be so nice but now you've turned into a 'stuck-up bitch' and a bunch of other colorful terms."

The woman chimed in, "We're all scared of him. You should be too. We get that you don't want to go the police, but you have to do something—if not for your sake, then for all of us."

They also mentioned that Smith's partner had been with him on one occasion and seemed embarrassed. They said this partner might corroborate my story.

My parents had been urging me to contact a close relative who was on the job. I had been resisting, saying there was no good way to do this. If someone ordered him to stop stalking me, he would obviously know I had complained about him. What would happen if I ever called 911? Would anyone come? There were many possible ways a cop could retaliate against an "enemy."

It was upsetting. I have cops in my family, and I'm a big supporter of law enforcement. The vast majority of police officers are well-intentioned and took this challenging job to "protect and serve" the public. But now I had come across one of the bad apples who give cops a bad name.

Anyway, I eventually felt compelled to call my relative, and he said it would be taken care of. He later told me it had been handled with a stern warning about possible charges and a transfer to a much tougher neighborhood. Lieutenant Smith never bothered me or my neighbors again. But the situation left me rattled.

I co-hosted News 12's morning show for three years, sticking around each day to solo-anchor the noon news. I also hosted a weekly talk show about current affairs called *Reporter Roundtable*. Produced by Robert Licata, it aired on weekends.

I had a nice gig at News 12, but I was hoping to move to a city station. I would send out a résumé tape now and then, but I didn't have enough time to make a serious push. As usual, I was busy and focused on doing a good job, day to day. It was like running on a treadmill. I was feeling a little trapped.

Back then, the assignment editors screened all calls. One day, Kim came to my desk and said, "Ummm…Don Hewitt is on line two for you?"

I rolled my eyes and chuckled. Don Hewitt? The legendary producer of CBS's *60 Minutes*? I doubt it.

I assumed it was one of my friends playing a prank. In the past, I'd gotten calls from pals using Hollywood-style accents, saying,

"Hello, Patti Ann, Katie Couric is sick today. We need you to fill for her!" *Ha ha.*

But just in case, I stayed professional. I picked up the phone.

"This is Patti Ann Browne. May I help you?"

"Patti Ann! Don Hewitt here."

My heart skipped a beat. I had seen him interviewed, and I could tell from his voice and tone that it really was Don. Freaking. Hewitt.

"Hellow!" I said, in an overly journalistic voice.

"So I watch your show on weekends when I'm on Long Island," Don said. "I have a house in the Hamptons. I never miss *Reporter Roundtable.* It's interesting! I said to my wife, Marilyn, 'This girl is good!'"

"Why, thank you," I replied. *Was that a British accent I was using?*

"I'd like to bring you in to the network for an interview," he continued. "We don't have any openings as far as I know, but I'd like the CBS brass to meet you anyway. Can I set it up?"

That was the beginning of the end of my tenure at News 12.

Now, mind you, Mr. Hewitt wasn't talking about the local CBS affiliate in New York. He was bringing me into the *network.* It would be a huge jump from News 12.

I didn't get a job at CBS. I did go in for interviews with several of the heads of the network's news division. The interviews went well but, as Don had noted, there were no openings.

However, I used the opportunity to hire an agent, who leveraged my CBS News interviews to get me network-level interviews at ABC and NBC. NBC News was hiring for its recently started 24-hour cable network, MSNBC. I was given a three-year deal as a full-time update anchor. I had jumped the fence from local news to network.

CHAPTER 7

Fox on the Run

MSNBC's studio was in Secaucus, New Jersey—just across the Hudson River from Manhattan. Unlike News 12, which was only seen on Long Island, MSNBC was a network—seen across the nation and around the world.

MSNBC aimed to make news more appealing to the younger demographic, so the studio was a far cry from the traditional sets I was accustomed to back then. The various anchor desks were scattered around a cavernous working newsroom. It was "warehouse chic"—modern and industrial, with brick walls and hip lighting. Every time I stepped into that studio, I felt cool.

The "MS" in the name was for Microsoft—NBC's partner in this venture. A new thing called the "World Wide Web" was gaining momentum, so we did a lot of stories about the internet and whether or not it would impact our lives.

I started out doing hourly headline updates ("cut-ins") on the overnight shift, but my first few updates each night were actually during late prime time, on *The News with Brian Williams*. The studio was bustling with excitement during prime time. Brian was always joking around with everyone, creating a fun and laid-back atmosphere. But once his show ended, most people went home, leaving behind a skeleton crew to cover the graveyard hours.

I anchored cut-ins every hour or so until the morning, catching short naps in between when I could. That's the difference between local cable and network news. Having written all my own stuff up until that point, it seemed like an incredible luxury to have a producer writing my updates. I worked with him, of course. I gave my opinions on what we should be covering, and I copyedited every script.

If a big story broke in the middle of the night, it was all me. Not wanting to be scooped by the other networks, the producers would throw me on the set the second something happened, regardless of whether we had any details at all. I did a lot of ad-libbing. If we didn't know anything, I would literally talk about what we didn't know.

"We don't know if there are any survivors. We don't know why the plane went down. We don't know if it was a mechanical issue, or perhaps terrorism. We do know the weather at the time was...."

Even talking about what we didn't know held viewers' interest. My job was to buy time until our producers could get more information and get guests booked. I had covered a lot of breaking news during my years anchoring at News 12, so I had some practice in stalling. But without sound bites, guests, or commercial breaks (they were killed during breaking news), I had to be talking nonstop, which made it impossible for me to do any news gathering of my own. I relied on the producers to feed me information in my earpiece.

I tried to glance down at my computer while I was live, scanning for more information. But I had to exercise extreme caution before reporting anything that popped up on the computer. Attribution was essential. I had to tell the viewers where the information was coming from and emphasize that we had not independently confirmed it.

If I was lucky, the producers were able to book a guest for me—typically a "phoner." Of course, the guests usually didn't know much yet either, so we spent a lot of time in that danger zone of hypotheticals.

This would go on for an hour or two, until Brian could get back to Secaucus after being awakened from a sound sleep. Brian was MSNBC's "go-to guy" for breaking news. (This was long before he was caught exaggerating on air.)

By the time Brian took over, more staff had arrived, guests had been booked, and producers had gathered a lot more information. On-screen graphics had been created, and sometimes there were even scripts written for him. It gave the appearance that there was a stark difference between my coverage of breaking news and Brian's coverage. Brian was very skilled at breaking news, and I learned a lot from watching him. But it was also a matter of timing. Brian had the benefit of an extra hour or more of preparation by an entire staff. I was flying blind.

I was happy to be promoted off overnights after a year. My new gig was weekend show host and daytime cut-in anchor three weekdays. Being the solo host of a two-hour show on Saturdays and Sundays was great exposure. Every Sunday morning, I had the privilege of interviewing Tim Russert, the highly-regarded host of NBC's *Meet the Press*, live on my show. I also contributed to the prime time newsmagazines *Special Edition* and *Headliners and Legends*. And working under the NBC umbrella, I was asked to fill in once in a while as update anchor on the business network, CNBC.

As an NBC employee, I got to rub elbows with some network bigwigs like Conan O'Brien, whom I met at a party at "Rainbow

& Stars" at 30 Rock. I also chatted with Charles Grodin, Hoda Kotb, and Ann Curry at various times in the MSNBC green room. Outside the studios, I was a guest at galas like the American Celtic Ball and Concern Worldwide's "Seeds of Hope" dinner. And I was honored to be Aide to the Grand Marshal of the Glen Cove St. Patrick's Day Parade.

Among the biggest stories I covered as an MSNBC anchor were the Elián Gonzalez raid, the plane crash that killed John F. Kennedy Jr., and the Monica Lewinsky scandal. I started to notice that my politics were different from those of most of my colleagues. Those differences became more pronounced over my time at MSNBC. I had a few tense conversations with producers regarding editorial slant, and I found myself watching the upstart rival cable news network, Fox News Channel, in my down time.

I rarely socialized with co-workers. For one thing, my hours were not conducive to that. But also, after my experiences at News 12, I was determined not to mix work and my personal life. So at MSNBC, I kept to myself. I enjoyed chatting with anchor Jodi Applegate and some of the behind-the-scenes folks, but for the most part, I did my job and left. This new strategy may have saved me from heartache, but I'm not sure it served me well in terms of getting along with colleagues. MSNBC didn't feel like "home" the way my other jobs had.

With a few months left on my three-year contract, I told my agent, Gregg Willinger, that I wanted to move to Fox News. Several of my MSNBC colleagues had already made the jump across the river, and they all reported back that working conditions were better there. So Gregg called the executive at Fox who screened applicants. The exec hadn't heard of me and wasn't interested in seeing my tape. Gregg called me and broke the news, saying that was the end of that.

I was disappointed. "Really? That's it? There's no other way in?"

"No," he said. "He's the guy agents reach out to."

I tried to come to grips with the fact that I would probably renew with MSNBC for another three years, even though I was pretty miserable there.

About a month later came another one of life's blessings in disguise—*deep* disguise. MSNBC informed me that they were not renewing my contract.

This really shouldn't have been a surprise. It was obvious I didn't belong there. But I had never been let go from a job before. I was always considered a stellar employee. It was a pretty devastating blow to my ego. It was also scary, since I now owned an apartment in Manhattan. I needed a job—one that could pay my co-op mortgage and maintenance.

I called my agent and asked him to call Fox again. Gregg said there was no point. He would just be transferred to the same guy who had said no a month earlier. I said, "Try anyway."

He called and was told the exec was out on medical leave.

Gregg paused, then asked, "In that case, can I talk to Roger Ailes?"

"Sure. Hold on."

A minute later, Roger, the CEO of Fox News, picked up and Gregg said, "I have this client over at MSNBC. Her name is Patti Ann Browne, and she really wants to work at Fox."

"I see her all the time!" Roger said. "Gotta keep an eye on the competition. When can she come in?"

Gregg said it was *that* easy.

The interview with Roger went well…and I guess I should note that it was completely professional. More on Roger in a later chapter, but getting back to the blessing: if MSNBC had renewed my contract, we never would've made that second call to Fox News. I would have committed to three more years at a job that clearly was not a good fit.

Instead, when my contract ended at MSNBC, I embarked on the longest and most fulfilling phase of my career—Fox News Channel. They say when God closes a door, He opens a window. In this case, I might say He closed a window and opened a door.

On a warm July day in the year 2000, I left my apartment on the Upper West Side and hopped on a subway, headed to my first day at Fox News Channel. A few stops later, I emerged in Times Square. Looking up at the familiar neon signs and tall buildings, I felt an incredible thrill. I *worked* here now. Never before had I lived and worked in the same place. At WSJV and MSNBC, I didn't even live in the same *state* as my job. For my other jobs, I drove long distances every day from Queens to Nassau and even Suffolk County on Long Island.

But now I lived and worked in a city often described as the center of the world. And Times Square is considered the center of New York. This was my stomping ground. I felt the energy as I walked the two quick blocks to the News Corp building. I was surprised by my own emotion.

It was a new decade, a new century, and I had a new job. I felt exhilarated as I entered the building and was escorted to the elevator. Exiting on the 17th floor, I walked down the corridor past the offices of Bill O'Reilly and Shepard Smith. I got to my own office.

My name plate was already on the door: Patty Anne Brown. They spelled all three names wrong. Oh well, it couldn't be *that* perfect.

I checked the view from my floor-to-ceiling window: blue sky above, Times Square below, the glistening Hudson River beyond. It was beautiful.

I had brief meetings with producers, executives, and the wardrobe department. My short "Katie Couric" hair, which NBC had loved, would have to be grown out. Fox women had long hair. And my annual wardrobe allowance would be used by the network's fashion consultants to purchase clothes in brighter colors and more flattering cuts. I was issued a pager so I could be brought in for breaking news. (A few years later it would be a Blackberry, and then an iPhone.) I was shown the studios, which looked familiar to me from my days of watching Fox at home.

Back in my office, I sat at my desk and logged onto the computer to familiarize myself with Fox's internal news system. A guy from the computer help desk had taught me how it all worked. Across from my desk was a closet that would soon be filled with suits and dresses. Next to the closet was a bookcase with a TV on one shelf, tuned to Fox News.

That office would be my second home for almost 18 years.

The next day, perched in a high swivel chair in the Studio B greenroom, a robe draped over my anchor outfit, I flinched when my makeup artist, Iren Halperin, aimed a pair of tweezers at my eye.

"Sorry," I apologized. "What are you doing?"

"Oh, these are false eyelashes. You didn't wear these at MSNBC?"

No. Here I was thinking the process of preparing to go on-air had been long and meticulous at MSNBC. At Fox, it was like getting made up for your wedding, every single day. It took about an hour and a half to get my hair styled and makeup done each morning.

But I didn't mind. It gave me a chance to chat with the hair stylists and makeup artists, and with other anchors or guests getting done up in adjacent chairs. I would also spend some of that time reading up on the day's news. On days when I hosted shows, I prepped for guest interviews.

When I would finally look up from my notes and into the mirror, the transformation was stunning. Although the anchors were referred to as "the talent," there was plenty of talent off-camera—especially on the Fox makeup and hair team.

I looked so different with my on-air hair and makeup that there were times when my colleagues literally didn't recognize me without it. I came to work each day with damp hair and no makeup so the artists could start with a blank slate. Walking down the hall with my frizzy hair, pale eyelashes, and red cheeks, I'd say hi to people I regularly worked with. My greeting would be met with a confused "Hey..." while the person shuffled away awkwardly. It dawned on me that these folks had no idea who I was. But once I had my "Fox look" on, I'd pass the same people again, and they'd say, "Hey, Patti Ann, how are you?!" seemingly unaware that we had already greeted each other hours earlier.

I also noticed a difference in how I was regarded by strangers. In the morning, walking from the subway to my building, covered with face cream and no makeup, no one would look my way or say hi (which was fine). But when I left work after my shift, fully glammed up, it was remarkable. Men working in the street or just passing me on the sidewalk would say, "Hello! Have a nice day!"

Apparently only pretty girls deserve nice days.

I started out doing cut-ins every half hour during Fox's daytime lineup. I also sometimes anchored prime time cut-ins—during *Your World with Neil Cavuto*, *Special Report with Brit Hume*, *Hannity & Colmes*, and *The O'Reilly Report*. I even occasionally anchored headline updates during *Fox News Sunday*, which aired on the Fox broadcast network.

Before long, I was guest-hosting on weekends with Eric Shawn or Todd Connor—both good guys. After a year or so, Brigitte Quinn and Linda Vester started taking maternity leaves, and I filled in for them as weekday host for months at a time.

People often asked how early I'd arrive to host a show. The answer is at least four hours before air time. There was no rule. We didn't punch a clock, and some anchors cut it closer than others. But I liked to prepare as much as possible. Sometimes, the night before, I'd tell friends I needed to get to bed because I was anchoring early the next morning.

They'd say, "I thought you weren't on till 9 AM."

"Yes," I'd say. "That means I have to wake up at 4 to leave my apartment by 4:30 to get to work by 5 AM."

Some people seem to think anchors just roll out of bed and onto the set, but that is not the case.

I'd get to my office and call the show's producer. Sometimes there was an in-person meeting of everyone involved in the show, sometimes just a conference call. Other producers just spoke with everyone individually. We'd go over the rundown—usually a mix of "readers" (short stories where the anchor is on camera), VO/SOTs (the anchor talks over video and then tosses to "sound on tape" of someone speaking), live shots (tossing to correspondents out in the field), and guest interviews.

I would head to the green room for makeup and hair. In the chair, I would read the papers and get caught up on the stories of the day. Back at my desk, I would scroll through the AP feed to see the very latest headlines and copyedit my show scripts as they were written.

But the bulk of my prep time was spent getting ready for guest segments. These were in-depth live interviews with one or more guests. Sometimes I was moderating a debate between a Republican and a Democrat on a contentious political topic. Other times I was interviewing just one guest, often an expert on a subject in the news, like a medical issue. No matter what it was, I had to be familiar with the topic.

I would plan a bunch of questions in advance, but I had to be ready to go "off script" based on the guest's responses. The segments were only three to four minutes long, which went by very quickly, especially if the guests were long-winded. I'd have to make judgments on the fly as to whether or not it was worth following up on something the guest said, knowing it would mean I wouldn't get to some of my other questions. Sometimes it would go very smoothly. Other times my interviews just didn't flow. No matter how it went, I had to shake it off. Tomorrow would be a new day, and I would hopefully learn from whatever went wrong today.

It was important to be upbeat on-air, no matter how I felt inside. This was challenging if I was tired or if things weren't going well in my personal life. I had to fake a smile and make it look sincere so it felt genuine to the viewers. But I realized something after a while: smiling on the air, even if it was just "acting," elevated my mood. Pretending to be happy actually made me happy. I noticed this time after time.

There are a few studies that back up my observation, and others that don't. Some psychologists say it's unhealthy to act happy if you're sad inside. But at least for me, the "facial feedback theory" holds true. It postulates that smiling tricks your brain into thinking you're happy, thus triggering a physiological response that makes you happy for real. It definitely works for me.

The hosting put me in the spotlight a lot more than doing cut-ins. And I discovered that the spotlight isn't always good. For a while, I was co-hosting a lot with Shepard Smith. Suddenly I started getting angry e-mails asking if the rumor was true—was I "having an affair" with Shep?

Someone obviously made this up to manufacture a scandal to damage the Fox News brand. But whoever came up with this brilliant scheme did not do their homework. There were so many holes in this baseless accusation, I hardly know where to begin.

For starters, Shep is gay. (He is out of the closet, so I'm not revealing anything my friend hasn't made public.)

So secondly, to be clear: no, Shep and I never dated. He's a smart and fun guy, but obviously not my "type."

But thirdly, Shep and I were both SINGLE when this rumor was circulating. I didn't even have a boyfriend at the time. The word "affair" suggests infidelity. Even if Shep and I *had* dated—which we did NOT—there would've been absolutely nothing wrong with it. Fox does not forbid interoffice dating. In fact, there have been many marriages between Fox co-workers. So the word "affair" didn't even make sense. This was a blatant attempt by a Fox News detractor to smear a couple of its anchors. And it was an epic fail.

Yet, *was* it a failure?

Not entirely. As I mentioned, I got e-mails asking me to "confirm or deny" the rumor. I was advised to ignore the e-mails. The theory is that any time a "celebrity" issues a denial, the denial gets a lot of press, thereby publicizing the rumor to people who hadn't already heard about it. And inevitably some of them will believe the rumor despite the denial. Best to ignore it rather than spread it even further.

But that advice didn't even apply in this case, since neither of us was married. People just assumed we were. I got an angry letter (in the actual mail) from one woman who said, "You make me sick! You pretend to be all wholesome and sweet, and meanwhile you're out there cheating on your husband! I know it's true because you haven't denied it! You disgust me!"

I guess it's too much to ask that people do a little basic research before believing every stupid thing that someone writes on the internet.

Another person e-mailed me to say, "It must be true because I'm seeing it everywhere on the internet."

When will people realize that anyone can write anything online, and if it's juicy enough, it will spread? The frequency with which a rumor is repeated online is not a measure of the truth of that rumor. It's just an indication of how scandalous the rumor is.

The more shocking the story, the more likely it is to be repeated. Yet people still claim, "Where there's smoke, there's fire!" Well, no. Actually, where there's smoke—especially on the internet—there is often a troublemaker with a smoke machine.

So being semi-famous had its downside, but most of my fans were wonderful. In the days before Twitter and Instagram, people posted frame grabs of their favorite TV personalities in Yahoo Groups.

One computer-savvy fan from Alabama named Marc Brewer started up a group in my name which he generously called "Brains and Beauty."

He e-mailed me first to ask if I'd mind. On the contrary, I was flattered! He spent time uploading photos of my anchoring, and people were allowed to comment under them. Marc, as moderator, insisted on respect and removed any inappropriate comments. It was really nice, and the group had thousands of members before things started shifting to Facebook and other social media.

Marc and I ended up e-mailing back and forth quite a bit. He would confirm my on-air schedule every week so he could post it in the group, and we would get to talking about other things. Before long, he went from "fan" to "friend," although we never met in person. We still send each other funny birthday cards and are friends on Facebook.

Other fan groups popped up in my name, prompting Marc to ask me to designate "Brains and Beauty" as the "official fan site of Patti Ann Browne." I obliged, and put a link to it on my own web site, which gave some people the impression that I had named my own fan group "Brains and Beauty." As if! Trust me, my opinion of myself is not that high.

After several years as moderator, Marc got too busy to run the group, so he passed the torch to "Mike Malone" (not his real name) in North Carolina. Mike was someone else who became a friend. We e-mailed regularly, writing about basically everything that was going on in our lives. He was like a pen pal, and some of my emails to him were more like diary entries. As with Marc, I have not yet met Mike in person, but I still consider him a dear friend. It's amazing how well you can get to know people through correspondence.

Once things moved to Facebook, I got to know even more fans. Although most Facebook comments are short, they reveal a lot. I paid attention to posts about my on-air segments. Most people were happy with my interviews, but the ones who weren't provided useful insights into where I fell short. I took those comments to heart and kept them in mind for future guest segments. Viewer feedback can be hurtful at times, but constructive criticism can make an anchor better.

The positive feedback is much appreciated as well! You might assume that people who work in television have thick skins, but that's often not the case. I've found that most anchors are sensitive types who internalize the negative comments. So we are very grateful to see supportive posts. We might not always respond individually, but that encouragement gives us the strength to keep going when it feels like the world is beating us down.

After my first three years with Fox News, my contract was renewed. By that time, I was doing even more substitute hosting. I co-anchored *Fox & Friends* with Steve Doocy and Brian Kilmeade a few times, filled in on the prime time *Fox Report*, and co-hosted countless daytime and weekend shows.

One of my friends commented, "You pop up everywhere!" It was sort of true. In addition to appearing on the 24-hour cable channel, I also did airline updates (short newscasts that would play on US Air seatback screens during flights) and gas station updates (news at the pump).

I also showed up occasionally on the Fox broadcast network. Separate from the cable channel, the broadcast network is the one everyone's familiar with. It's made up of affiliates around the country, such as Fox 5 in New York. The affiliates broadcast a mix of sitcoms (such as *The Simpsons*), dramas (like *911*), reality shows (like *The Masked Singer*), and sports. Each affiliate airs its own local news, but they run FNC's network news program, *Fox News Sunday*, on Sunday mornings.

By contrast, Fox News Channel is a separate 24-hour news network shown across the US and around the world on cable and satellite. That's the one I was usually on. My relatives in Ireland regularly watched me on FNC. I even heard back from a friend who moved to Australia.

Since each Fox broadcast affiliate produces its own local news programs, they sometimes "borrow" reports from Fox News Channel to cover national or international stories. So as an FNC employee, I was sometimes asked to record in-house reports for Fox News Edge—the affiliate service that provides news pieces to Fox broadcast stations nationwide. So my friends would sometimes catch my reports on the Fox 5 local news.

Now and then, a news story broke that was so big it warranted interrupting whatever program was airing on the broadcast network. For example, when Michael Jackson died in 2009, I did a network break-in from the Fox News Channel studio, cutting into the popular show *TMZ* with a "Fox News Alert" to announce the King of Pop's death.

Whenever I appeared on the broadcast network, I heard from a few friends. They'd say, "You are *not* going to believe this! I was sitting in my living room watching Channel 5, and YOU came on!"

Did they think I was lying when I said I was a TV news anchor? I learned that a lot of my friends never watched Fox News Channel, but they were evidently big fans of tabloid gossip shows like *TMZ*.

I got a pretty good sense of where my friends stood politically when I made the switch from MSNBC to Fox News Channel. Living in Manhattan, a notoriously liberal city, I felt comfortable telling people I worked for left-leaning MSNBC. But when I moved to Fox, I avoided telling people what I did for a living.

I met a man at a party and told him I worked for Fox News Channel, and he responded, "And you're comfortable doing the work of Satan?"

Even some of my own *friends* didn't hide their disappointment in me for moving to "the dark side." They were impressed when I worked for MSNBC, but now that I worked for Fox, they saw me differently, even without watching my actual appearances.

On the other hand, much to my surprise, when I switched to Fox, some of my long-term friends from the city quietly "outed" themselves as conservatives. I had never discussed politics with my Manhattan friends. The city is only 10 percent conservative, so I assumed my friends were in the other 90 percent. They assumed the same thing about me, so we all stayed mum. We listened to the liberal viewpoints all around us and kept open minds, but when we disagreed we were reluctant to speak up, since the numbers were against us.

But now that I was with Fox, my friends decided it was safe to let me know they were conservative. Several of them whispered to me, "Fox News is my favorite channel. I'm so glad you're there."

I was surprised to discover that I had inadvertently made friends with a lot of conservatives without even knowing their politics. Of course, I also had many liberal friends, and I continue to respect their views. But the number of conservatives in my circle was statistically improbable given the demographics of Manhattan. It seemed that the conservatives had unwittingly gravitated toward each other.

I'm not conservative on every topic. On certain issues, I'm more of a moderate. Nonetheless I realized I had been biting my tongue for years—at work and at play. Since media organizations are overwhelmingly left-leaning, I had rarely spoken up about politics at my previous jobs. And since New York is liberal, I hadn't felt comfortable expressing my views in my social circles either.

That had changed now, and it was like a weight off my shoulders. I was still in the minority politically, but I had finally found others, at my job and in my personal life, who saw things the way I did.

I loved working for Fox. I felt comfortable there. I liked my co-workers, and they seemed to like me, which was not the case at MSNBC.

And the hours at Fox were more reasonable. I was even allowed to use my vacation and comp days. (A comp day is compensation for working a sixth or seventh day in a week.) At MSNBC, I was always told they couldn't spare me right now, because it was a "busy news cycle." It was an international network. There was always news breaking *somewhere*. So I frequently worked six-day weeks but could rarely take a day off for a family function, let alone take a week's vacation.

Once I was at Fox, I had a much better "work/life balance." Instead of ducking out of a party after an hour, I could stay till the end. I could take time off to attend weddings and even go on vacations.

And in 2002, Fox News Channel overtook CNN as the number one cable news network in the country—a position it has held ever since. So the producers and executives at Fox were generally in a much better mood than those at third-place MSNBC. My career, at least, was moving in the right direction.

CHAPTER 8

Musical Chairs

*"I tried to make so many relationships work
when it was obvious they wouldn't...I rolled
through every stop sign, ignored every red flag."*

–Shannon Bream, *Finding the Bright Side*

I laughed when I read those words in my former Fox colleague's memoir. They perfectly describe my own love life during what I call my "Decade of Dating," from approximately 1991 to 2001, spanning three jobs and three apartments.

My romantic life was all over the place. In short, well-meaning friends told me I was too picky and I was throwing away good men. So I started accepting dates from nice guys who had great "resumes," even though I wasn't feeling chemistry. I tried, but you can't talk yourself into having feelings for someone, no matter how perfect they may seem on paper.

Giving up on that strategy, I moved into a disastrous "bad boy" phase. Since dating guys who were ostensibly my type wasn't working, I figured I'd try dating guys who were completely wrong for me. (Not married men or anything like that—just men with whom I had nothing in common but to whom I felt an attraction.) Not surprisingly, that didn't work either. It was a roller-coaster decade of highs and lows....

After my three relationships with cameramen (one in South Bend, two at News 12), I started to get serious with a software designer during my last few months at News 12. I met Rich through my volunteer work with the Interfaith Nutrition Network on Long Island. He worked in Manhattan and lived in Long Beach. My early hours at News 12 were inconvenient, but we managed to work around them. However, once I moved to MSNBC, it was a challenge.

After each grueling overnight, I would drive home from New Jersey to my apartment in Queens, where I slept most of the day. Rich and I basically gave up on seeing each other during the week. On weekends, I tried to rally so we could spend quality time together, but it was difficult to "reset" for just two days each week, only to reset again when Monday rolled around. He was mad at me for sleeping so much and for being grumpy when I was awake. I was mad at him for being mad. It didn't work out. Truth be told, there were other issues, and I do believe things happen for a reason.

By coincidence, we ended up seated next to each other on a train many years later. I was surprised to learn he and his wife live in the next town over from where I live with my husband and son. It was nice to catch up.

After Rich, I had no shortage of suitors, but I wasn't finding the man I could see myself marrying. I did have some good times with friends.

Early on, I shared an apartment in Queens with my twin sister, Colleen. When she got married two years after our younger sister, Mary Lou, I rented an apartment by myself. My Queens apartment complex was popular with young professionals because of its proximity to a train to the city and to a strip of bars where there was a lively night life. We called our apartment complex "Melrose Place," because it reminded us of the TV series by that name from the 1990s. Mary Lou and her husband, Jim, lived there after they first got married, as well as a bunch of my cousins.

We continued the tradition started by my high school gang of playing co-ed flag football in the park on weekends. I was a terrible player and broke five fingers during my football years, but I loved those games. Afterwards, we'd have pizza at a pub or go back to someone's apartment to hang out and watch more football.

I also ran in lots of 5K (3.1-mile) races for charity. I never joined another track team after scarlet fever forced me off my high school team as a freshman, but I kept on running recreationally. It was a lifelong passion. It lowered my stress and kept me fit. I loved running.

In the Northeast, the thing to do over the summer if you're single is to rent a share house in a beach town. So during college, I spent fun summers in cramped houses in Long Beach with my high school gang.

After graduating, one of my first shares was in the Hamptons with my cousins from the "Melrose" apartment complex and their friends. That summer, I was working weekends at News 12, which made it difficult for me to be at the house when everyone else was. My housemates all worked in the city, so they came out on Friday nights and left Sunday evening.

I took some days off so I could be there for weekend barbecues, but I also enjoyed staying there during the week. The house had a tennis court and a hot tub and was near the beach. It was relaxing being there alone on weekdays. And it wasn't a much longer drive to my Long Island station from there than it was from my Queens apartment.

I wasn't always alone. My housemates would take days off during the week. And my cousin Ed Tracy's friend lived nearby and was working that summer as a caddy at a golf club a few miles away. Known by most of us simply as "Axe," he wanted a job in finance and said the caddying gig was great for networking. So Axe would sometimes show up at the house on weekdays. We'd have lunch or dinner in the yard and drink a few beers. I would jokingly remind him that he did not have a share in the house, but he knew I enjoyed his company. He was funny and obnoxious in the most respectful way, if that makes any sense.

Axe went to Fordham, as did I, but he was a few years younger, and we didn't know each other in college. But I started bumping into him at Fordham alumni events. Just when I'd be getting bored, I'd spot him and think, "Oh, this is going to be a fun evening after all!"

Eventually, as Axe had hoped, a connection he made while caddying got him a great job at a brokerage firm in downtown Manhattan. He moved into the city and started joining our group in Queens for our weekend football games and nights out. We all went skiing a few times up in the Catskills. Axe even invited our group to watch a basketball game from his company's luxury box at Madison Square Garden. Axe and I never dated, if you're wondering, but he was always a good time.

The following summer, I was in a different Hamptons share with two girlfriends and a bunch of people we didn't know. We were trying to expand our circle. But taking a share with strangers is always a roll of the dice. Some of the people in this house were great. But others were not my type.

I fell asleep "early" one night (around midnight) and when I awoke in the morning, I went to look in the mirror before exiting my room. The mirror was gone. I asked the group at breakfast if any of them had seen my mirror. One of the women said she borrowed it. I said, "Oh, your room doesn't have a mirror?"

She said, "No, it does, but mine won't come off the wall."

Confused, I asked, "Why did you need to take a mirror off the wall?"

She glanced at some of our fellow housemates and they all snickered.

"Oh, Patti Ann," she said. "You're so naïve."

A friend later explained that they needed the mirror to snort cocaine. Never tried it. Never will.

Two of my relatives passed away before their time due to drug addiction. As a result, I'm very wary of drugs, including prescription narcotics. If I'm in excruciating pain after an injury or medical procedure, I'll take *half* of one pill. If the pain is still unbearable when that wears off hours later, I'll take another half. As soon as I can get by with just Tylenol or aspirin, I do that, even if it doesn't entirely eliminate the pain. I don't mess with drugs. I've seen how they destroy lives.

Once I got the job at MSNBC in Secaucus, I switched to summer shares in Spring Lake, a nice town on the Jersey coast. The boardwalk was a beautiful spot for morning jogs, and I made some good friends in those houses.

But when the summers ended, most of the people I met through my share houses went back to their Manhattan apartments. They continued to get together in the city, but since I lived in Queens and worked in New Jersey, it was a hassle for me to commute into the city for a few hours and then take the train home late at night.

Meanwhile, the fun group from my Queens apartment complex eventually dispersed. The married couples had kids and moved into houses, and many of the single people got married and moved too.

It seemed that if I wanted a social life as a single woman now in my 30s, Manhattan was the place to be. So, I bought a one-bedroom apartment on the Upper West Side. The rents in the city were so high that it made more sense to pay a mortgage.

I loved living in Manhattan. I jogged around the reservoir in Central Park or on the path along the Hudson River. I joined a recreational volleyball league (NY Urban Professionals) and even found another co-ed flag football league (Yorkville Sports) to play in.

The dating scene picked up again once I was living in the city. But things didn't always go smoothly.

My cousin set me up with a guy who checked all the boxes. He came to my apartment to pick me up, and he looked handsome in a nice blazer and button-down shirt. On the street outside my apartment, he tried to hail a cab, but sometimes there are no cabs to be had. (This was before Uber.) I told him I didn't mind taking the subway. But he insisted on finding a taxi, and was eventually able to flag one down.

It was the cab ride from hell. As a New Yorker, I'm well aware that most taxi drivers seem reckless at times, but this was way beyond the usual cabbie aggressiveness. I'm fairly certain this driver was high on drugs. He was speeding and weaving, blowing through red lights, and forcing pedestrians to leap out of his path to avoid being hit. Then an ambulance came up behind us, one lane over. Its lights and sirens were going, so everyone cleared out of the right lane to let the ambulance whiz by.

Well, our cabbie saw this empty lane as his opportunity to beat the traffic. He pulled right in front of the speeding ambulance, forcing it to slam on its brakes.

I yelled, "There's an ambulance behind us!"

He seemed surprised and yanked the cab back into its previous lane, narrowly avoiding an accident.

I wanted to get out, but I took a few deep breaths and tried to relax.

But then a second ambulance came along, lights and sirens blazing, right where the first one had been. Again, everyone cleared out of the lane. Again, our insane cabbie jumped *into* the empty lane, directly into the path of the speeding ambulance. Again, I yelled, "Ambulance!"

Again, the ambulance slammed on its brakes, and again, our cabbie pulled back a millisecond before we were hit.

I whispered to my date, "Can we get out? I'm not comfortable with this driver."

My date replied, "No. It took us too long to get this cab. We'll never get another one."

I said, "We can walk."

He said, "It's too far to walk."

I pleaded with him, still in a whisper, "Then let's take the subway. Please!"

He looked highly offended and said, "No date of mine is taking a subway to dinner! I'm a gentleman."

I see. So a "gentleman" doesn't let his date take the subway, but a gentleman *does* disregard his date's clearly articulated wishes and literal fear for her life. I felt helpless.

I was wearing a seat belt, and I urged him to at least put his on. He said no because he didn't want to crease his snazzy blazer. Still doing all the wrong things to make a good impression on me.

I sat there gripping a handle on the door, praying for the ride to end. We were going *so fast*, in thick traffic.

Then BAM! We ran a light and crashed hard into a car crossing the intersection. My date's head slammed into the divider between front and back seat. He screamed, "Ow!!!"

The front end of the cab was crushed. Since I was belted, I was fine. But my date was holding his head, and I must admit it was difficult for me to summon up sympathy for him under the circumstances. I was furious but kept it to myself.

I asked if he was okay. He responded, "My head hurts!"

Yes, well, if only he had respected my wishes and let us exit the cab, he'd be fine! Even if he'd worn a seat belt as I'd suggested, he'd be fine.

I said, "Well, it looks like we're getting out of the cab after all!"

Miraculously, no one was seriously hurt. But the taxi was destroyed, as was any chance of romance with this guy. He and I had different definitions of "chivalry."

Living in Manhattan, I was meeting lots of wealthy 30-something New Yorkers. I was going to fancy parties and fundraisers, and my share houses were usually with very successful people. Some were very down-to-earth. I met many warm and genuine people during those years. I'm still in touch with some of them.

But when we mingled with my friends' acquaintances from their wider circles, I sometimes felt out of place. I could hold my own with the upscale Manhattan crowd when necessary, but I didn't always enjoy it. Some of them were pretentious. I had a share house with a wonderful group in Newport, Rhode Island, one summer. But when we went to their favorite nightspots, I'd hear women whispering in the ladies' room about some woman's tacky purse or shoes, or the fact that she was wearing "last year's skirt." Perish the thought!

A believer in buying American, I drove a new Buick Regal. It was a great car, and nice-looking. But at one of my Spring Lake share houses, where the driveway was mainly full of BMWs, a housemate suggested that in the future, I park my Buick in a lot across the street, since our driveway was "crowded." I pointed out that I was usually the first to arrive at the house, so if anyone should be parking across the street, it should be her. We are *not* still in touch.

In the city, I found other single women in their 30s to hang out with. One adventurous friend decided to try out this new fad called "online dating." The rest of us thought she was crazy, until she told us she was getting serious with a man she met through Match.com. He didn't seem real to the rest of us. He was "that guy from the internet," as though he resided in the computer and didn't actually exist in real life.

When we finally met him, we were shocked. He was nice-looking, well-spoken, had a good job, and treated our friend well. (They later got married and now have kids.) We all decided to check out Match.

Wow! It was like ordering from an à la carte menu. You simply checked off the boxes for what you wanted, and profiles of guys who met your specifications popped up in your inbox. My married friends were jealous. This seemed to make dating so much easier! Meeting someone in a bar is a crapshoot. Online, you place your order, and your ideal mates are delivered to you on a silver platter.

Not exactly. I will say I met some great guys through Match.
com. Back then, only people who were looking for serious relationships were willing to put themselves out there in this new, exper-
imental forum. So the men I met were sincere, and I had no bad
experiences. But I didn't make a love connection, I sometimes got
recognized from TV, and I discovered some harsh realities.

First of all, a lot of guys "misrepresented themselves," to put it
politely. (I'm sure many women did as well.) And secondly, I found
that many men are not interested in dating women their own age.

I'm not sure how Match works these days, but back then, you
would fill out a multiple-choice profile stating your age, religion,
political leanings, and so on. You would then check off the criteria
you were looking for in a mate. If you didn't care about a certain
category, you could check "no preference."

So I submitted my criteria, and Match sent me the profiles of
guys who matched them. And if I met those men's specs, my profile
popped up in *their* inbox too.

I assumed that if a man matched *my* parameters, I probably
matched *his*. So I didn't contact the guys I found interesting on my
list of matches. Being old-fashioned, I would wait until the men
contacted me. Very often, they did.

But there were a few who didn't. One was a guy who I already
knew in real life. (I actually saw lots of familiar faces on Match.)
But this acquaintance came up as the #1 match for me, based on
the criteria I had specified. I was surprised and yet not. I had always
felt a bit of chemistry between us, but he had never asked me out. I
figured maybe he would now.

Nope. I began to wonder if he even saw my profile. It was possible that I didn't come up as a match for him based on his criteria, even though *he* came up as a match for me based on mine. So

I checked his profile and found out I was right. This guy was six years older than me, but I was above his chosen "age range." He was in his 40s but only willing to date women in their early 30s or younger. So I didn't even pop up as a match for him. He never knew that Match found us compatible in every other way. He inadvertently dismissed me due to my "old age"—which, again, was *six years younger than his*!

A few years later, when I was engaged to my husband, Mike, we threw a party and the guy was there. A few drinks in, he congratulated me on my engagement and said, "You know, I always regretted never asking you out. I don't know why I didn't."

I smiled politely and said, "I'm too old for you."

He said, "What? You're a lot younger than me."

I said, "Yes, I am. And you came up as a top match for me on Match.com, but I was above your age range."

He looked puzzled and crestfallen.

"You were on Match?"

"Yes, and you came up as my #1 most promising prospect. But I never even showed up on your list, because you refuse to date anyone who's even close to your own age."

He gasped, "Well I certainly would've dated *you*!"

I shrugged and said, "Oh, well," and walked away to join my younger fiancé.

I was an early adopter of Caller ID. Back in the '90s, it was so new most people hadn't even heard of it. Or at least, they never thought anyone they knew would actually engage in the extremely devious act of secretly finding out who was calling them.

At the time, Caller ID was a separate box that you connected to your phone. It had a small display window. My box was labelled

"Caller ID," so I covered that with a piece of black tape and hid the box behind a picture frame next to my phone.

Oh, it gave me lots of laughs. Since the guys I dated didn't know I had it, it was enlightening to see how many times they would call and not leave messages. When I finally answered, they would pretend they just happened to catch me when I was home. One guy called nine times in one day.

Of course no one does that now, because everyone has Caller ID and everyone knows that. But back then, these guys assumed I had no way of knowing that they were calling me multiple times per day.

If any of my exes are reading this book, they're probably recoiling in horror right now, realizing I knew all along that they were the ones who left the hang-ups on my phone.

If I'm making it sound like I was always in the driver's seat, trust me, I wasn't. I broke some hearts, but I also had my heart broken many times during my years of dating. In fact, I seemed to have a unique gift for reuniting men with their exes. In several instances, guys I was dating broke up with me to go back to women who had dumped them.

"We need to talk," the man would say. "Remember that girl I told you about?"

"The one who took your heart and stomped on it?" I'd say.

"Yes, her. We're getting back together."

"What? How did this happen?"

"Well, it's funny," the guy would say. "I told her I was dating you. She got all freaked out. Then she called me the next day and said she wants me back." *Yes, that's hilarious.*

A friend told me I should consider it a compliment. She said it seemed like these women were jealous when they found out their ex was dating a "glamorous" news anchor. So I was doing these guys a favor by making them look more valuable in their ex-girlfriends' eyes. These men were ending up with the women they really loved, and their women now appreciated them more because of me. I was a regular female Cupid.

You're welcome, I guess.

Although I dated a lot, I wasn't sleeping around. As a single woman living in Manhattan, I totally appreciated a lot of the scenes in the TV show *Sex and the City*—the lists to get into parties, the cabs, the various types of men with their dating styles, the mistakes the women made, the obsession with fashion. Some of the scenes really cracked me up.

But after an interview with Helen Gurley Brown, I mentioned to her off-camera that the show was very relatable to me as a single Manhattanite, "except I'm not having all that sex."

The author of *Sex and the Single Girl* and long-time editor of *Cosmopolitan* magazine looked at me with concern and said, "Dear, why on earth not?"

Although I was a typical city girl in many ways, I was no "Samantha."

The singles scene sometimes got me down. But I've noticed that when you start to get too wrapped up in your own problems, life tends to hand you a wake-up call regarding what's important. My family suffered losses during the '90s. My grandmother on my dad's side, Bridie Browne, died at age 85 after suffering for many years with Alzheimer's disease. Grandma was a warm and loving woman who took great care of her family. It was very difficult to watch her brain and body slowly waste away. As tough as it was for me, it was even tougher for my dad and my grandfather.

Granddad passed away eight years later at 89. Their lifelong love for each other served as a great example to me during my single years. At their funerals, I reflected on how much they overcame, immigrating to America as teenagers, building a life together from scratch, struggling to fit in at a time of anti-Irish sentiment in New York. They had no time to sweat the small stuff.

I, on the other hand, sometimes felt sorry for myself simply because I wasn't married, instead of looking at all the blessings I had—a great career, good health, a nice apartment, good friends, and a strongly supportive family, which grew to include two fantastic brothers-in-law and four wonderful nieces. Although I was often the "seventh wheel" with three other couples (my parents, my sisters and their husbands), we had so much fun together.

My brothers-in-law liked to joke about my love life. My mom had a framed photo of my sisters and me with our "men": Mary Lou's husband Jim, Colleen's fiancé Mike (yes, my twin and I both married Mikes), and my boyfriend at the time. Luckily, my boyfriend was on the end, because when he became an "ex," my mom simply cut him out of the photo and stuck it back in the frame, leading Colleen's Mike to joke, "Note to self: always stand in the *middle* of a Browne family photo!"

Another time I stopped by my parents' house after a date. Mary Lou and Jim were there and asked where I had been. I said I was at a nice new restaurant, and I gave them the name. And then I said, "But I just dumped the guy."

A few weeks later, Mary Lou suggested to Jim that they have dinner at that same restaurant. Jim said, "No way! I know what hap-

With parents &
twin Colleen
(PA is on right.)

Patti Ann, Colleen, Mary Lou

In Communion dress before
it was torn in half (Chap. 2)

Water-skiing in Hamptons

WFUV-FM (Fordham) with Kathleen Biggins

Reporting for NYIT (Credit: *New York Tech*)

The living room "antenna tree" (Chap. 4)

Anchor/News Director of TV 55 LI

WSJV-TV 28 South Bend, IN (Chap. 5)

News 12 on-air images provided by News 12 Long Island

Interviewing NY Gov. Mario Cuomo

Ad on Nassau County buses (with Joe Cioffi, Carol Silva, Bob Wolff)

Fox News—the early days

With Glenn Beck

Fox Fan Day at Yankee Stadium: Tucker Carlson, Peter Johnson, Heather Nauert, Brian Kilmeade, PAB, Steve Doocy

All Fox News Photos—Credit: Fox News Channel

Red Eye: Greg Gutfeld, Bob Beckel, Kurt Loder, Bill Schulz, PAB

With musical idol Pat Benatar (Chap. 11)

5 AM Show Hosts: Heather Nauert, PAB, Heather Childers, Ainsley Earhardt

Engaged to Mike, 2003 (Chap. 9)

Wedding Day, May 1, 2004

With sisters & parents

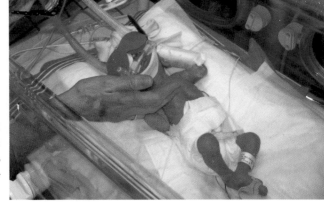

Connor in NICU shortly after his birth 11 weeks premature, weighing 2 lbs. 6 oz.

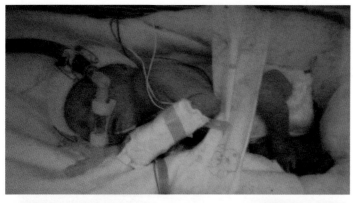

From 82 tough days
in the NICU to
happier times

First time at
the ocean

Connor & Hunter

Draw a picture of one thing your parent does at work.

L: Connor's drawing of Mike giving a child a shot (Chap. 10)

Connor playing tuba

Below L: Mike, Connor & PA all finished a triathlon.

Below R: Connor jumping off sailing ship during Scout trip.

Mike & Colleen, Mike & PA, Jim & Mary Lou, 2021

With Mike's family in Hawaii (Credit: *Kris Labang 2018*)

Hamptons 2021: Connor is much taller than PA!

pens when Browne girls take men to that place—you won't catch me in that Dead End Café!"

These two funny guys are like the brothers I never had.

Our whole family liked to gather over the summer at my parents' house in the Hamptons. After saving for years, my parents had purchased their dream home on the water. It had lots of bedrooms, so my sisters and I could all come out with our families. We would ride on my parents' boat, water-ski, barbecue, relax at the ocean, and swim in the pond.

We also started heading down to the Florida Keys every February during President's Day week. We went on sunset sails, kayaked through the Everglades, and swam in our rented condo's pool. Married or not, these were happy times.

I remembered the advice of my former co-anchor Carol Silva. Carol was already married with kids when we worked together, and she loved family life. But she urged me to embrace the opportunities I had to focus on my career and enjoy life as a single woman. She predicted that I would miss the freedom once it was gone. So when I started to feel blue, I tried to appreciate having the independence and resources to make the most of my single years.

I went to Disney with some girlfriends from News 12, went back a few years later with my mom and cousin Kara, and even flew back to Ireland with a friend from one of my share houses.

I went to a ton of Broadway plays, rock concerts, and comedy shows. I caught jazz at Joe's Pub. I enjoyed New York Philharmonic concerts from a blanket on Central Park's Great Lawn, and I went to the ballet, the opera, and choral concerts at Lincoln Center.

There were also sporting events; I saw the Mets, Yankees, Rangers, Jets. My buddy from WFUV, Jim Morganthaler, got me great seats at the US Open every year. I saw some of the greatest tennis players of all time at Flushing Meadows.

And my good friend Ray Mastrangelo had season tickets to St. John's basketball games at Madison Square Garden. One of his friends rarely used his ticket, so I would take the subway down from the Upper West Side to meet Ray at the Garden. Ray will tell you I rarely paid attention to the games. I just "blah-blah-blahed" in his ear the whole time, cheering when the fans in red cheered. Those were fun days.

Just over a year into my time at Fox, I celebrated my birthday at a bar in the city with a bunch of friends. We had a fantastic time. So many of my friends from various circles showed up—from my share houses, my volleyball and football leagues, my church, my job, even old friends from Fordham. I went home to my apartment that night feeling very happy.

My birthday is September 10th. When I awoke the next morning, it was September 11th, 2001. And the city was about to change forever.

I was at Fox when the planes hit the Twin Towers. I was in my office preparing for cut-ins. Jon Scott was anchoring on my TV. After the second plane hit, Jon was saying there was now little doubt that this was terrorism. Manhattan was seemingly under attack. I was in shock.

Axe worked on the 103rd floor of the World Trade Center.

My cut-ins were cancelled, but I stuck around, figuring I'd be asked to report on some element of the crisis. Luckily, I wasn't asked, and I didn't offer, as I normally would, because I was having a great deal of trouble processing what was happening. Many of my colleagues were jumping in, so I kept my head down. The thing about working for a network is that the anchors come from all around the country. I was one of the few "locals" on the air at Fox. So I knew people in those towers. Many of my on-air colleagues did not.

I went to seven funerals in two months. Axe was gone. His name was John McDowell, Jr. We also lost former News 12 cameraman Glen Pettit, frequent Fox guest Barbara Olson, and Teddy Brennan from my Spring Lake days. My good friends lost siblings, parents, spouses, friends.

It was a terrible year. In New York, there was a pervasive sense of loss and vulnerability. Nearly everyone knew someone who died in the towers. And the incident exposed the fact that Americans could be attacked on our own soil. It shattered people's sense of security. I was now living and working in Manhattan, and every time a plane flew overhead, it sounded too close. I tried to fight my fear, knowing fear is the precise goal of terrorism. But I ended up seeing a therapist for panic attacks.

But most of all, I was grieving. Losing Axe, especially, was a devastating blow to his fiancée, my cousins, our friends, and to me. And my pain was nothing compared to that of others who lost family or best friends. And it's not over yet. Sixteen years after 9/11, Mike's cousin Mark passed away of an illness related to his exposure to toxins while working near Ground Zero. The 9/11 attacks continue to take lives to this day, more than two decades after the planes hit the towers. I will never forget.

The following year, Colleen and I made an interesting discovery. We had gone more than 30 years believing we were fraternal twins, since that's what the doctor said when we were born.

"Fraternal" means the mother dropped two eggs into the womb when she was ovulating, and they were each fertilized by a different sperm. Two separate eggs plus two separate sperm equals separate DNA. So fraternal twins are no different from ordinary siblings except that they were born at the same time. They can look nothing alike, or they can look very similar, as with most siblings.

But identical twins are created when the mother drops only one egg, and it's fertilized by one sperm. For reasons unknown, the fertilized egg splits in half early on, creating two separate embryos with the same exact DNA. This makes them genetically "identical."

Fraternal twins have become more common as fertility treatments induce more eggs to drop, and due to in vitro fertilization. And fraternal twins often run in families. (The tendency to drop more than one egg during ovulation can be genetic.) But there is no genetic tendency to have identical twins. The splitting of a fertilized egg into two embryos is completely random and more rare, occurring in only 0.3 percent of all births.

For most of our lives, people were skeptical when Colleen and I told them we were fraternal. Not only did we look extremely alike, we also had the same mannerisms, the same habits, and the same way of speaking.

One summer during college, I was at a party talking to a guy who knew both Colleen and me. We were chatting for quite a while—close to an hour—when he said, "So how's Patti Ann?"

What? The entire time we were talking, he thought I was Colleen. Awkward!

Even Colleen's daughters, when they were young, would come up to me and say, "Mommy…" then look up embarrassed upon realizing, "Oops, you're not my mom."

We're sometimes asked if we have a "psychic connection." When one of us is injured, does the other one feel unexplained pain? Do we know if the other twin is happy or sad at any given moment?

No, none of that has happened. But we can certainly read each other like a book when we're together, and even when I'm on the air. Once I was anchoring a cut-in on MSNBC while Colleen and my mom chatted on the phone.

"Oh, no," Colleen said, glancing at her television. "Patti Ann has a migraine."

"What?" my mom said, checking her own TV. "She looks fine."

"No, look at her eyes. She has a bad headache."

My mom called me later and asked how I was feeling.

"I have a terrible migraine," I told her. "I'd rather not stay on."

"Wow," my mom said. "Colleen was right!"

And there are tiny things, like buying the same cards for each other on our birthday, or both of us buying the same card for our parents. We also seem to end up with the same brand and shade of lipstick, but that's partly because we have the same coloring. Still, there are thousands of lipsticks in the world, yet we'll both pull the same exact one out of our purse.

Once DNA testing became widespread, I read an interesting article. It said DNA testing of twins had revealed that a third of twins who were declared fraternal at birth were actually identical.

Before DNA testing, the method used to make that determination was very unscientific. The obstetrician basically examined what came out with the babies. If it looked like just one placenta, the babies were identical. If it looked like two, they were fraternal. But in reality, the article explained, the "afterbirth" usually gets ripped up in the birthing process, so what might look like two placentas is often just one, torn in half. So doctors erroneously conclude that the twins are fraternal.

And this was happening *a third of the time*!

I called Colleen and said, "I would bet good money that we're in that third!"

She wasn't as excited as I was. I wanted to get a DNA test, but she didn't see the point. She said it wouldn't change anything, and she was fine believing we were fraternal.

I understood, and we set it aside for a bit. But later she changed her mind. She realized the question was medically relevant. If I were allergic to a drug, chances were Colleen was, too, and maybe her kids. And it would determine whether her daughters were genetically predisposed to have twins themselves.

She called me and said, "Let's do it."

We told our parents and Mary Lou that we were getting the DNA test. Our mom and younger sister told us we were wasting our money. There was no way we were identical. They both knew us so well; they didn't see us as alike at all.

"You're totally different from each other!" Mary Lou insisted.

Our mom agreed, "You're nothing alike!"

She also clung to: "The doctor said fraternal!"

Well, we did the cheek swabs and the result came back: identical!

Mary Lou and Mom were shocked. Dad wasn't surprised at all. And everyone else said, "Of course you're identical."

Colleen and I weren't sure how we'd react to this news. I found myself feeling really happy about it. I'm not sure why. It didn't change anything, but to me, it's kind of cool. I was afraid Colleen would be disappointed, but she was happy too. It felt good to know the truth   a truth we had probably both known deep inside all along.

Although Colleen and I were now proven to be identical, our lives looked very different at that point. Colleen was married with children, while my love life was starting to feel like a game of musical chairs. When the music stopped, everyone else seemed to find their spot with someone, and I was left standing, chairless. My fun group of single girls kept shrinking as they married one by one. I was truly elated for all of my girlfriends, but I was becoming less optimistic about my own chances of finding true love.

For most of my life, things had worked out best for me when I stopped worrying and had faith. My most successful strategy was not to focus on what I wanted, but rather focus on what I had, take care of daily business, and leave the rest to God.

But that wasn't what I was doing when it came to love. At some point during my single years, my faith foundered. People mentioned "biological clocks" and asked, "Why aren't you married yet?" as though finding a soulmate was a task I should've checked off my list by now. I was left with the impression that love was something I had to go out and get. It wasn't simply going to "fall into my lap," I was told. So I had been trying too hard. That's probably why it didn't happen for me during my Decade of Dating.

It was time to "let go, let God."

CHAPTER 9

Cool Roman Catholics

"Happiness is like a butterfly: the more you chase it, the more it will elude you, but if you turn your attention to other things, it will come and sit softly on your shoulder."

–J. Richard Lessor

I decided to stop chasing love. I turned my attention to my job, my friends, and my family. I was at peace with myself.

I also resolved to stop making foolish choices, like dating men I could never see myself marrying. One of the rules I had imposed on myself toward the end of my Decade of Dating was to stop dating younger guys. They were a lot of fun, but they were not in the same place in their lives as I was.

So back in the late '90s, when Christine Tracy, my cousin Ed's wife, asked if she could set me up on a blind date, my first question was, "How old is he?"

She told me his age. He was more than five years younger than me, which was my new limit. I said forget it.

But Christine, a doctor at a hospital in Manhattan, persisted.

"He's much older than his age. He's a doctor. He works with me. He's very mature."

I said I appreciated her trying, but I was through with younger guys.

"I don't know," she said. "For some reason I can really see you two together. You're both Irish Catholic…. I just have a feeling about it."

I stood my ground. "I'm trying to be more realistic about the men I date."

Plus, my previous blind dates had not worked out. And then I literally said, "If I happened to meet and fall in love with someone that much younger than me, that would be different. But it seems like a waste of time to go on a blind date with a stranger who's so much younger. He'll take one look at me and say, 'Wow, she's old!'"

"Patti Ann, you don't look your age," Christine said. "I didn't even realize you were that much older than he is. But okay, never mind."

And that was the end of that. A brief conversation at a party that was quickly forgotten. She never even said his name.

Once I moved into my Manhattan apartment in the late 1990s, I became very involved in my Catholic parish. I was attending Mass every Sunday at Holy Trinity Church on the Upper West Side, a few blocks from where I lived. I usually went in the morning, but fortuitously, I ended up at the evening Mass one Sunday. As it wrapped up, a couple of 30-something guys, Frank Gonzales and Dave Cervini, made an announcement from the altar. Frank said something like this:

"For those of you who aren't aware, some of us have started gathering after Mass. A while ago, my friend Ron and I noticed that there were lots of young professionals in the

pews, attending Mass alone. We were thinking we'd like to meet them, and maybe they'd like to meet us. So we invited our fellow parishioners to meet us at a nearby bar after Mass so we could get to know each other. It has become a popular tradition, so if anyone out there wants to join us, meet us outside on the steps, and we'll go across the street to the Firehouse for a few drinks."

I figured, why not? So I joined about 30 young men and women as we made our way to the Firehouse Tavern around the corner. I had a great time. Some of the others had been gathering for months, but they welcomed me to the group.

The Sunday night 5:30 Mass became a new habit for me, followed by the Firehouse, where we all met for drinks and camaraderie. We were grateful to Frank and Ron for coming up with this idea, and to Dave for taking charge of the group. We were also glad our pastor, Monsignor Thomas Leonard, gave them the green light to extend the invitation.

When it was time to give our group a name, Dave came up with "CRC," which stood for "Contemporary Roman Catholics." But we all called ourselves the "Cool Roman Catholics" which, in hindsight, probably proved we were anything *but* cool.

Dave started organizing other events for the CRC: sleigh-riding in Central Park, swing dancing lessons, Super Bowl parties, bike rides for charity, even a white-water rafting trip. I participated in almost all of them. After 9/11, we got busy collecting and sorting donations for the workers at Ground Zero.

Needless to say, romances started to blossom. The CRC was never billed as a "singles group," and we all valued it for the wonderful friendships that were formed. But there's no denying that it also provided the opportunity for single people to date others who had at least two things in common: we lived on the Upper West Side, and we were Catholic.

I've lost count of how many couples who met through the CRC have since gotten married. It's a high number. Personally, I went on one or two dates with quite a few of the CRC men. They were all great guys, and it was worth a shot, but after a few dates we'd go back to being friends.

I spent a lot of time with the CRC, but on summer weekends, I was usually at my share houses. In the summer of 2002, I had a share in a beach house in Spring Lake, New Jersey, so I attended Mass down there every Sunday during the summer months, missing Holy Trinity's after-Mass gatherings.

When that summer ended, a CRC friend, Brian Wycliff, had a bunch of us over to his apartment one day to watch football. The topic of conversation turned to a guy my friends were calling "Doctor Mike."

They were saying Dr. Mike was finishing up his residency and spending a lot more time with our group. Having not been around for about three months, I had no idea who they were talking about.

"Who's Doctor Mike?" I asked.

"Doctor Mike?" my friend Anne Carol Winters said. "You must know him. He's been hanging around with us for months! He's tall, good-looking, has wavy hair...Doctor Mike!"

I shrugged. "Doesn't sound familiar. I haven't met him."

Apparently, I had somehow managed to avoid the newest addition to our group. He had been at some CRC events that I'd missed, and I had been at others that he'd missed. Our paths had not crossed.

One of the guys commented, "He's very young, actually. I'm not sure why he hangs out with our group. We're sort of the older faction of the CRC. I'm surprised he's not spending time with the younger gang."

Suzanne Roccisano chimed in, "Maybe he just likes older people. He seems like an old soul. Some people enjoy spending time with a more mature crowd. After all," she joked, "we're very smart and sophisticated."

It turned out Suzanne knew Dr. Mike well. They met at a CRC event and discovered they both loved partner dancing. They started attending a weekly dance night in the city and got really good at "ReJive." Also known as "modern jive," it's a lively dance that combines swing, salsa, and hustle. Suzanne and Mike danced so well together that they entered a jive dancing competition and came in second. Mike even taught some ballroom dance classes.

I was becoming mildly curious about this mysterious Dr. Mike, but not as a romantic prospect after hearing his age. It would just be nice to match a face with the name. But for another three months, my work hours prohibited me from attending the CRC nights out. The phantom Dr. Mike receded to the back of my mind.

Every December while I lived in the city, I threw a big Christmas party at a bar in my neighborhood. A lot of my Fox News friends attended, along with friends from share houses, volleyball, football, and the CRC. My goal was to have my friends from various circles meet and mingle. In fact, every year so far, a couple had met at my party and become a serious item. It was a track record I prided myself on, so I made it clear that all were welcome.

About a week before my party that year, Suzanne called me and said, "I just want to confirm…we *are* allowed to bring friends to your party, right?"

I said, "Absolutely! The more the merrier."

"Thank you!" she said. "I have to tell Doctor Mike you said that. I told him about the party, and he doesn't want to come because he doesn't know you, and he wasn't invited, and he feels like he'd be crashing."

"You tell Doctor Mike that he'd better show up at my party. The whole CRC is coming! Of course he's invited. I can finally meet him."

As the solo hostess of a huge party at an Upper West Side bar called the Parlour, I was very busy the night of December 5th, 2002. The party space was crowded, and I was moving from group to group. I remember glancing over at one point and noticing a handsome guy whom I didn't know talking to Anne Carol.

"This is great!" I thought. "There are some fresh faces here. That makes the party better."

A short while later Anne Carol came over with the handsome guy and said with a flourish, "This…is Doctor Mike!"

"Ah, the famous Doctor Mike!" I said. "Glad you decided to come! I've heard so much about you."

"Oh no," he quipped. "That can't be good."

I laughed. "I hear you're a great dancer."

He said sarcastically, "Uh, yes, I'm a regular Twinkle Toes," then looked immediately embarrassed, like he wanted to take it back.

I said, "Well, you and Suzanne should hit the dance floor and show off your swing dancing moves!"

Someone was tapping me on the shoulder so I said, "Have a great time. Nice meeting you!" and I was swept up in the crowd.

My party was early in the holiday season, so it was sort of a "kickoff" event. The following weekend, Anne Carol held a small Christmas party in her apartment. Mike was there. So we got to chat a little more that night.

The beer started to run out, and Anne Carol asked if anyone could go on a beer run. Mike was nearby and volunteered. I offered to go with him (you know, to help him carry it, because beer is heavy, and we had to walk to buy it since we were in the city).

Walking to the deli, I said, "So what's your deal? I know you're a doctor. What kind? Where do you work?"

He said he was a pediatrician and worked at a hospital in the city. I asked which one. He named the hospital.

"You're kidding. My cousin Christine Tracy is also a pediatrician at that hospital! You must know her!"

"Yup, yes, I know Christine," he said brusquely, then hurriedly changed the topic. "So what about you?"

I remember thinking it was odd—how anxious he was to get off the topic of Christine. *What was that about?* Did he and Christine not get along? Or, perhaps, did they date before she met my cousin Ed? Hmm.

We continued our conversation, and I found myself thinking he really was adorable, then chastising myself for the thought. Didn't I swear off younger men?

We talked a bit about computers, and I complained about the troubles I was having with mine. He said he was somewhat of a computer whiz and offered to come by my apartment to fix my computer settings. I blurted out something about having to buy him dinner in exchange. *What was I saying?*

He said, "It's a deal."

My mind was racing. *Was this a date?* Hard to tell. If it was a date, I'd have to say no, right? I had a rule! But it really wasn't a date. He was just fixing my computer, and I was paying him with dinner. Strictly a business transaction. In that case, it was fine. Of course it was fine.

I agreed.

A few days later, I did my hair and put on a cute but casual outfit for this "business transaction." He really was good with computers, and managed to solve most of my longstanding problems. Afterwards, we chatted and joked around. I said I owed him dinner, but he said it wasn't necessary. I thanked him and he left.

I stood inside my door blushing. *What the heck is going on?* I can't fall for a guy that young! Not to mention that handsome! This guy could date someone 15 years younger than me. I need to snap out of this! Besides, he turned down my offer of dinner. Clearly, he's not interested. Shake it off, Patti Ann.

But we kept bumping into each other. There were more holiday parties and CRC gatherings, and Mike and I coincidentally attended every one. And if a seat opened up next to mine, Mike always seemed to take it.

The night before New Year's Eve, our group from the CRC attended a Swing Ball at the Supper Club in Manhattan. The group was pretty evenly split between men and women, but not all of the men were dancers, so Mike was very much in demand. When I arrived, he was on the floor with Suzanne, and they were amazing!

I had always loved swing dancing, although I never got great at it. During my Decade of Dating, a married friend suggested I make a list of qualities my "ideal man" would have. It sounded silly to me, but she insisted it was a helpful exercise to articulate exactly what you're looking for—even the less important things. This way you know it when you find it. So, I made the list, and one of the items was: "*Likes to dance, especially swing dancing.*" It was way down at the bottom, because I hardly knew any men who enjoyed swing dancing, and I was certainly prepared to give that up.

But there was Dr. Mike, spinning Suzanne around the floor, clearly enjoying himself.

"*You've gotta be kidding me,*" I muttered to myself.

After taking a turn with a few other gals from our group, Mike extended his hand to me. I felt very self-conscious as he led me out onto the floor. I had taken the first round of swing dancing lessons with the CRC, so I knew a few basic steps, but not nearly as many as Mike. However, he was a great lead—easy to follow even without knowing the moves in advance. We danced around the ballroom under the lights of the mirror ball. It felt magical.

As the ball dropped in Times Square to usher in 2003, I was still trying to push Mike out of my mind. I had been hurt enough times to be afraid to fall in love, and this felt scary. I was definitely getting the sense that Mike had a crush on me, but crushes pass. Remembering the men on Match.com who wouldn't even date women *near* their age, I figured Mike would never consider dating someone older. Even if he did, there was no way we would work out as a couple. He would eventually succumb to the charms of a much younger woman, leaving me behind with a broken heart.

But Mike was fully a "member" of my social circle now, so there was no avoiding him. He even joined the CRC volleyball team I organized. We were getting to know each other pretty well.

In February, Dave Cervini set up a "CRC Spring Break" in Jamaica. A bunch of us signed up for it, including Mike. It was great to escape the winter with a group of friends. We snorkeled, relaxed in the sun, and had poolside drinks at an all-inclusive resort.

There were some women there from what we called "the younger faction" of the CRC, and a few seemed to have their eyes on Mike. Wearing cute little bikinis, they hovered around him, laughing at his jokes. I tried not to notice and told myself I didn't care, but I was obviously jealous. It made me realize I had it bad for this guy, despite my denials.

I felt a little better when I noticed that Mike seemed to be rebuffing the advances of these other women. In fact, he was spending the bulk of his time with me. And we were having witty, flirty conversations.

Finally, Steve, a CRC guy whom I had briefly dated, pulled me aside. He was on the trip with his new girlfriend. He asked what the deal was with Mike and me.

"What do you mean?" I asked, trying to sound breezy. "There's no deal."

"Come on, Patti Ann. Everyone thinks you two are dating. Are you?"

"No," I said. "I'm sure he'll end up with one of those younger girls who are throwing themselves at him."

"Are you crazy?" Steve asked. "Mike has been following you around like a puppy dog this entire trip. He's not interested in those other women. You've gotta get over the age thing."

"I'm scared," I blurted out.

"Patti Ann, love involves risk. Stop fighting it. You two obviously have chemistry. You'd make a great couple. You deserve love."

I'll always be grateful to Steve for that pep talk.

During that trip, Mike asked me out to dinner. "Just the two of us...a date," he made clear.

I said yes.

Mike and I quickly became an exclusive couple. We told our CRC friends we were together, and most of them said, "Haven't you been dating since last year?"

At Fox one day, I was getting my hair done when my stylist, Carol, thanked me again for inviting her to my Christmas party at the Parlour. She said she had a great time. Then she said, "Hey, so who was the couple?"

"Which couple?" I asked.

"You said every year at your party, a couple gets together. Who was the couple this year?"

I thought about it, remembering who met last year and the year before. I couldn't come up with any couple that met at this year's party.

Disappointed, I said, "Huh, I guess the streak is broken. I haven't heard any reports of couples getting together at my party this year."

"Too bad," she said.

I stared at the mirror as she blow-dried my hair, then suddenly my eyes widened and I exclaimed, "It was me!"

"What?"

"I'm the person who met someone at my party this year! I met my boyfriend at my Christmas party! The streak lives on!"

"Well, it's about time you got something out of it!" she laughed.

I smiled and started planning ahead for my next Christmas party—oops, I meant *our* next Christmas party.

I met Mike's parents and sister about a month into our relationship. They were having St. Patrick's Day dinner on a Sunday at their home on Long Island, and I was invited for dessert. I was coming from my parents' Hamptons house, where my family and I had attended the local parade the day before.

Sunday morning, I baked a cake with vanilla icing dyed green and left it on the table in my parents' kitchen. I told my mom and dad that I was nervous about this meeting, because Mike's parents had expressed misgivings about my age. My parents tried to lighten the mood by making "old lady" jokes.

I asked if my outfit, a green sweater and jeans, looked "youthful enough."

My mom said, "Wait…" and pulled out a shawl with fringe on the ends and wrapped it around me and joked, "Perfect!"

My dad grabbed a decorative Irish walking stick, called a shillelagh, and said, "Hey, Patti Ann, you should walk in using this," and he hobbled toward me using the stick as a cane. We all cracked up.

Then I commented, "Is it hot in here?"

My mom joked, "Whatever you do, don't say that!" More laughter.

It was time to pack up the cake and leave. I looked at the table, where my cake was sitting under the skylight, and gasped. The green icing had melted off and was pooled in puddles on the sides of the cake. (I guess it *was* hot in there.) I took a knife and tried to put the icing back, but the cake came up with it, so now there were cake crumbs mixed in with the icing. It was a mess!

My mom and I were frantically trying to salvage it when my sister Mary Lou walked in.

"What's going on here?"

"The cake!" I stammered. "The icing...the crumbs...it's a disaster!"

"Forget it!" she said definitively. "It can't be fixed."

"But I have to bring something homemade! It's Mike's parents!"

"It's over! Buy something from the store," Mary Lou insisted, grabbing the sad-looking cake off the table and moving it to a counter.

I couldn't believe it. I wasn't even there yet, and things were off to a bad start.

I stopped at a supermarket on the way and picked up Entenmann's St. Patrick's Day cupcakes. Arriving at the door of Mike's family home, I rang the bell, cupcakes in hand.

Mike's mom opened the door, took one look at the cupcakes, and started laughing uproariously. I wondered if it was too late to run away.

"Erin!" she called to Mike's sister. "Look what she brought!"

A pretty young woman came to the door, looked at the cupcakes, and burst into hysterical laughter along with her mother.

I lowered my eyes in embarrassment and noticed that both Erin and her mom were wearing dress pants. Mike had told me to wear jeans. *This just keeps getting better*, I thought.

Mike came over with his dad—both in dress pants—and we all settled at the table, where Mike's grandmother Eva was already seated. She gave me a warm, sincere welcome. It made me feel a little more relaxed. My cupcakes were placed on the table next to a plate of cannolis that Eva had brought.

Erin finally explained, "Just before you got here, we were lamenting the fact that my dad gave up sweets for Lent. My mom and I were saying we always used to get those delicious Entenmann's cupcakes for St. Patrick's Day, but now we don't because of my dad. Then you brought them!"

"Oh! I'm so relieved! I thought you were laughing at the cupcakes. I baked a cake, but it…it's a long story."

"No, we love the cupcakes!" Erin assured me. "And they make much more sense than the cannolis. Who brings cannolis on St. Patrick's Day?" she teased Eva. "It must be Grammy's Italian half coming out."

Ah, so Mike was part Italian. I filed that away, trying to learn as much as I could about his family.

The dessert went fine after that, and once I was gone, Mike's parents told him that we seemed to be a great couple, and the age gap wasn't an issue at all. He was happy and so was I.

Mike and I were together all the time. We went out for dinners, strolled around Central Park, went ice skating at Wollman Rink, and danced at the wedding of one of Mike's pals from the jive dancing circuit. We went skiing in the Catskills, staying with Mike's relatives at the country home owned by his Uncle Dick and Aunt Ginny.

We went to Broadway plays, including *Man of La Mancha* and *Thoroughly Modern Millie*. We watched Misty Copeland dance with the American Ballet Theater at Lincoln Center before she became principal dancer. I still went to Mass every Sunday at Holy Trinity, but now Mike was by my side in the pew. No matter where we went, we almost always walked or took the subway instead of cabs—another way in which Mike and I were compatible.

One day, when Mike and I were chatting, I offhandedly mentioned a woman named Kirsten who was friends with my cousins, the Tracys.

Mike said, "I know Kirsten."

"Really?" I said. "How do you know Kirsten?"

"Your cousin Christine set me up on a date with her about four years ago."

I paused. *Four years ago?*

"Huh…. That's interesting," I said. "Four years ago, Christine tried to set me up with a doctor who worked in the pediatric ward at her hospital."

"It was me," Mike said.

Mind. Blown.

"Wait, so…you've known all along?"

"Yes," Mike said. I guess he had been waiting for the lightbulb to go off in my head.

"So you and I could've started dating four years ago!" Now I was beating myself up for saying no back then.

"No!" Mike said. "Four years ago, I was in the middle of my residency. I was working and studying and sleep-deprived and irritable and hating life. If you had met me back then, we probably would *not* still be dating."

So that's how he saw it. God recognized that the timing was wrong, so He didn't let it happen. The way I saw it, God had a plan and I thwarted it with my free will. But God didn't give up. He tried again four years later, throwing us back into each other's path. Either way, it sure seemed like fate.

And my cousin Christine should really start a matchmaking business.

Mike proposed to me seven months after we started dating. We were sitting on a blanket at Jones Beach, eating a picnic dinner and watching the sunset. We both love the ocean. He took out the ring. It was perfect.

A short time later, we flew out to Seattle so I could meet Mike's brother Brian, who lived there. It was a fun trip. A few months after that, Mike's parents invited my whole family to their home for a "meet-the-future-in-laws" gathering. My sisters, their husbands, and my nieces enjoyed talking with Erin, Brian, and Mike's parents and grandmother.

Our wedding, of course, was at Holy Trinity Church in Manhattan, where our romance had begun. Colleen was my maid of honor, and Mary Lou and Erin were my bridesmaids. My four nieces were flower girls. There was a lot of dancing at the reception. Mike and I spent much of the night on the dance floor, as did many of our relatives and friends.

We honeymooned in Hawaii, then moved into our new apartment. I had sold my one-bedroom pad for a good profit after owning it for just a few years. It had been a good investment. Planning to have children, we purchased a two-bedroom co-op not far from Holy Trinity. The second bedroom would hopefully become a nursery.

I told my doctor I had recently gotten married and wanted to start a family. She cautioned, "It might take a while. You're 38. You also have a history of endometriosis. That could complicate things."

Endometriosis is a condition that mainly afflicts women who haven't given birth before age 30. It can cause pelvic pain and also jeopardize a woman's pregnancy. So my gynecologist recommended that I have laser surgery to remove the endometrial tissue before conceiving.

I had the laparoscopy and was told to prevent pregnancy for three months afterwards while my womb healed. I followed that guidance and got pregnant a month later—just four months after the procedure. Mike and I were thrilled that it happened so quickly for us!

But as you know, my pregnancy didn't go well, and I'll always wonder if maybe I should've waited longer after the laparoscopy before trying. The surgeon had commented that she removed a "ton" of tissue with the laser, which left a lot of scarring behind. Maybe it needed more time to heal.

Most of the other factors known to increase the odds of premature rupture did not apply to me: I had never smoked, never had an abortion, and never had a sexually transmitted disease.

But another theory of mine is that I ate too much the day before my water broke at 24 weeks. The day before the rupture was Father's Day, so Mike and I were at a barbecue in my parents' yard. I was famished when we arrived, so I filled up on cheese and crackers. When the dinner was served, I certainly wasn't going to skip that, so I dug in. I remember feeling very full after dinner. But after a break, the desserts came out, and it all looked so good. My weight was on the low side for someone at my stage of pregnancy, and I was eating for two, so I figured there was no harm in stuffing myself.

I felt very uncomfortable that night, and the next day my water broke, and I was hospitalized. I asked the doctors if the rupture could've been caused by overeating. Every doctor I asked said they were not aware of any studies linking premature rupture to eating too much at one time.

But interestingly, another woman who had the same rupture at the same stage of pregnancy commented that she also "pigged out" the day before her water broke. So I'm just putting it out there. If you're pregnant, even if your overall weight is fine, you might want to refrain from over-indulging at any one meal. Maybe it puts too much pressure on the membrane.

But that doesn't explain my earlier bleeding. Of course, I was also "of advanced maternal age" at 39, which statistically increased my chances of giving birth prematurely. So maybe it was that, plain and simple. Mike and I had no choice. We started as soon as we could. But many married couples choose to wait before conceiving. My obstetrician had warned me that she knew far too many couples who regretted putting off parenthood so they could "enjoy their marriage." The delay made it difficult or even impossible to get pregnant when they were finally "ready." And sometimes, it led to lifelong complications for their children.

In any case, thank God, Connor survived my shortened pregnancy and his brush with death in the neonatal intensive care unit. Mike and I were now a family of three.

CHAPTER 10

"Amen, Alleluia"

The day after Connor's code blue, we called our church and asked if a priest would come to the hospital to pray over him. Our pastor and his associate were both unavailable, so they sent someone we didn't know who was visiting from another country.

When he arrived, I was sitting alone next to Connor's Isolette incubator in the far corner of the NICU. I saw him scan the room. I stood and waved. He walked toward me, passing other incubators on his way. He glanced briefly at Connor's Isolette, but surprisingly, his eyes didn't linger on it. He looked at me, introduced himself, and asked where my baby was.

"Oh," I said. "He's right there."

I pointed, and the priest turned to Connor's incubator. Then he looked back at me, confused.

I looked for myself and finally understood his confusion.

Connor was so small and flat against his bed that he was barely visible. His face was obscured by the ventilator tube and the tape holding it in place. His tiny body was covered by white gauze, sensor pads, tubes, tape, and his tiny diaper, leaving just a few hints of flesh peeking out here and there. The priest thought the incubator was empty—just a vacant crib with some cloth and tape and equipment in it.

I showed him Connor's eyes. The poor priest burst into tears.

"This is your baby?" he asked, incredulous, in a thick accent I couldn't identify.

"Yes, this is Connor."

Tears were streaming down his face. Clearly, he had never seen anything like this before.

"Is he going to be alright?" he asked, staring sadly through the glass.

I patted him on the back and said, "He's going to be fine, Father."

In my head I was thinking, "Well this took a funny turn. Isn't he supposed to be comforting me?"

I assured him that with his prayers and those of many others, Connor would be okay, if that was God's will. By prompting me to speak those words of faith and optimism, I realized he had, in fact, comforted me.

He said a few prayers, still struggling to contain his emotions. As he left, he said, "Your son will always be in my prayers."

I thanked him for his compassion. I wish I remembered his name.

Two days after the code, Connor was taken off the ventilator. The blood transfusion was alleviating his anemia, and his vital statistics were back on track. It seemed he had just gotten tired of breathing and needed a rest for a couple of days while the ventilator did the work.

But ventilators aren't good for lungs, and the doctor wanted him off the machine as soon as possible. Mike agreed, but I was terrified. What would happen once the tube was removed? Would he crash again? A nurse had told Mike that Connor's code had lasted

10 minutes. *Ten minutes of not breathing.* I could not watch him go through that again.

I asked everyone to double down on their prayers. Since Connor's birth, I had been sending out e-mailed updates to friends and family. Connor's name was mentioned in "Prayers for the Sick" at many churches, and was on the list in the prayer circles of my friends, and even friends of friends who didn't know Mike or me, as well as Fox News viewers. We will be forever grateful to all of you who prayed, and I frequently tell Connor of your love.

Mike and I watched while the doctors removed the breathing tube. It was uneventful, thankfully. But this wasn't a surprise. We'd been told there would probably be no immediate issues. It was more a concern that he'd tire of breathing again at some point down the road.

So we were back to the routine—Mike visiting whenever he wasn't working, me spending my days reading and singing to Connor in his incubator. I could tell by watching his monitor that Connor was soothed by my singing. He was especially partial to TV show themes. "Gilligan's Island" was his all-time favorite. But the nurses loved it when I sang my fave—Pat Benatar's version of "Tell Me Why," about how God created Connor for me to love.

A believer in positive visualization, I often told Connor about the fun things we were going to do in the future. Since Mike and I both love the beach, I described the ocean to him and promised to take him there when he was older. Then I would make my daily visit to the hospital's non-denominational chapel and pray that I'd be able to keep my promises to my son.

Connor still had frequent bradycardias (heart slowdowns)— usually at least five per day—and each one struck terror in my heart.

But simple stimulation provided enough of an adrenaline boost to jolt him back to normal, as long as we did it immediately.

Within a few days, I was allowed to hold him again in my rocking chair, still attached to his CPAP machine to stabilize his breathing. Eventually the CPAP was removed for short periods, and then longer.

In all, he spent 82 days in the neonatal ICU. It was a roller-coaster ride, but thankfully it never got as dark again as day 16. He developed reflux and was visibly pained whenever my milk hit his stomach through the feeding tube. Medication provided some relief, but it was still an issue. He also developed a MRSA infection and was moved to isolation, where he remained until discharge. For weeks, we had to wear isolation gowns when visiting him.

Because I started pumping breast milk immediately after I delivered, I was pumping more than enough milk into plastic containers to keep up with Connor's needs. In fact, I told the nurses I'd be happy to give the extra to some of the other babies whose moms were distraught over not producing enough for their preemies. But understandably, this was strictly forbidden by health rules.

In time, Connor advanced from the feeding tube to taking my breast milk from a bottle. Eventually we tried breastfeeding. He did well the first few times, but then he struggled. Newborn preemies are too weak to latch, and by the time they're strong enough, it's sometimes past the "window" for them to instinctively know how. After a few sessions with a lactation consultant, I ended up alternating between breast and bottle, because the breast-feeding left him frustrated, and he didn't need added stress. But I felt good knowing he was at least getting my breast milk either way, since it's much easier for preemies to digest.

Once Connor seemed stable, a nurse recommended that I go back to work while he was still being cared for in intensive care, to save some of my maternity leave for later. It was clear I would need to be home with Connor full-time for a while after he left the hospital.

So I returned to Fox, a different person from the one who had left. It was weird being back at work. Between the bed rest and the maternity leave, I'd been away for months. My hair was still short, and I was clearly preoccupied with what was going on in the NICU. I wasn't following the news as closely as usual. I also had to pump milk in the middle of my shift. Seeing that I was not at the top of my game, Fox moved me off television for a bit and let me anchor updates for Fox Radio Network. I was grateful. The radio studio was in the same building on a different floor, and the people were great. Besides, radio was my first love.

As soon as my shift ended, I would buy food from the concourse under our building and eat it on the subway to the hospital to save time—something I never would have considered doing before, but I wasn't going to waste time sitting at my desk eating when I could be with my son.

When Mike and I were both at work, my mom stayed with Connor. She would bottle-feed and hold him. The nurses taught her how to revive him using stimulation methods such as yelling his name, rubbing his feet, or patting him on the back. There were a lot of babies in the ward, and sometimes the nurses were busy with others when Connor's monitor started beeping. After the code blue, it was imperative to us that someone be with Connor as much as possible to respond quickly to alarms. It was such a comfort knowing my mom was with him. It was a long commute for her to the hospital, but she was there for her grandson almost every day.

Finally, right around his original due date, we took Connor home. He weighed six pounds, 11 ounces and looked like a full-term newborn, round and pink. We thanked the NICU nurses, most of whom were loving guardian angels during Connor's 12 weeks in their care. They waved goodbye as we rolled him down the hall in a stroller.

He was wearing a portable version of his hospital monitor. There were sensor pads attached to his chest, with wires that ran to a machine that sat in a shoulder bag we carried with us everywhere. It would beep loudly if he had a "brady" or apnea event. We were taught how to attach the pads, and we had to sign a contract saying we understood that we had to respond within 10 seconds every time the monitor beeped. We both had to be certified in infant CPR. As a doctor, Mike already was. I took a course at the hospital.

Literally the second we arrived at our car on discharge day, Connor's monitor beeped—one of several alarms that first day. I was already wondering if it was a mistake to take him out of the hospital. The following day, in our apartment, his alarm went off 11 times. Eleven times in one day! We were glad to have him home, but it was apparent that this was going to be a bumpy ride.

My mom basically moved into our apartment, sleeping on an air mattress in the room that was supposed to be Connor's nursery. Connor slept in a bassinet next to Mike and me, so we could respond immediately to alarms during the night.

One night the alarm went off, and I jumped up but Mike remained sound asleep. This was a shock. The alarm was extremely loud by design. Until then, it had always awakened both of us. But we were exhausted. So now I had a whole new worry.

The next morning, I told Mike he'd slept through the alarm. He wasn't concerned. He pointed out that I woke up for it, so all was well.

"But what if we BOTH sleep through one?! If we both sleep through an alarm, Connor dies!"

He responded, "You'll never sleep through his alarm. You're his mom."

Three mornings later, he told me I had slept through an alarm.

"Now I'm afraid to sleep at all!" I said.

Nights were busy. Someone had to wake up for the overnight feeding, and again to change or comfort Connor when he woke up crying. I had to get up at least once overnight to pump, to keep up my milk supply. This also required bottling the milk and sterilizing the equipment after each pumping session. The whole thing took close to an hour. And, of course, we had to get up to revive Connor when his alarm went off, sometimes multiple times per night. Mike and my mom did some of the overnight bottle feedings, since I was pumping. It seemed like all three of us were up all night, and we were tired.

And now we were worried that our exhaustion could lead to our son's death. Thankfully, at least one of us awoke for every alarm. But it was a difficult time. Connor wore that apnea monitor 24/7 for 10 months. It came with us everywhere we went. We had a party in our apartment so our friends could meet Connor. It was a bit of a scene when the alarm went off and we revived him. It was routine for us, but quite the buzzkill for our guests. Fortunately, it was resolved quickly.

Meanwhile, our dog, Hunter, was back with us now, after months with my aunt and uncle. He quickly learned that the thing to do whenever the alarm went off was to run to Connor as fast as possible and hover directly over his face. He was a very helpful dog.

Over the months, the number of alarms tapered off, until we were finally able to give the monitor back when Connor was more than a year old.

I pumped breast milk for a year. We rented a large electric pumping machine. A device I called my "fembot bra" had big tubes coming out of both cups, enabling me to pump both breasts simultaneously. Mike walked in on me once and declared dryly, "I've never wanted you more." Luckily for him, I laughed.

I also had a smaller, portable electric pump which I carried with me everywhere. Between the pump, a cooler bag and ice packs to keep bottles of freshly pumped milk cold, the bulky heart monitor, and the regular diaper bag, we were not traveling light. It was almost not worth going anywhere.

Since I was breastfeeding, I continued to forego alcohol and caffeine, as I had during pregnancy. Giving up alcohol for two years was no biggie. I barely missed it. I definitely enjoy having a few drinks when I'm out with friends, but if I had to give it up forever, I'd be bummed for a day and then move on.

The caffeine part, however, was difficult. The crazy hours of the news business had gotten me hooked on Diet Coke. The hours caring for a newborn with special needs were even crazier. I constantly craved caffeine. But I certainly didn't want any unhealthy substances flowing into my baby. Connor had enough to deal with.

Finally returning the "balls and chains"—the heart monitor and the breast pump—was liberating. Even better, Connor was now a year old and doing well.

Therapists from New York State's Early Intervention program came to our apartment a few times a week to help him meet developmental milestones. He was a bit delayed with some of them, but on time with others. Perhaps due to my incessant talking and reading to him in the hospital, he was extremely verbal from an early age. His first word was "Doggie!" directed, of course, at Hunter. True to his Gaelic name, Connor loved his hound.

Connor's head was consistently tilted to one side—a condition known as torticollis. The doctors explained it was due to the lack of fluid in my womb after the membrane rupture. He was "swimming in shallow water" for a month, bumping up against my pelvic bone, forcing his neck and back into a twisted position. If not corrected, torticollis can lead to various problems down the road. So I took him to a special therapist for a few months, and we did home stretches multiple times each day, gently pushing his neck in the other direction, and used special supports to keep his head straight in his crib and car seat.

There would still be stormy weather ahead, but we'd made it through the worst of the rain. My parents told us they went outside during Connor's code blue, after my second panicked phone call, and saw a rainbow. At that moment they felt in their hearts that Connor was going to be okay.

They were right.

When Connor was 10 months old, we held a "blessing ceremony" for him at our church in Manhattan. The "official" Baptism had been done by Mike in the hospital, but Holy Trinity allowed us to go through the motions and say prayers of thanks. The ceremony was followed by a Christening party at Mike's parents' house on Long Island. It was a joyful day—for us and for all our relatives, who had clearly been worrying and praying right along with us during all those long months.

When Connor was a year old, we took him to the ocean for the first time. I had described it to him over and over when he was in the NICU, saying, "That's where Daddy and I got engaged, and you're going to love it." I was trying to stay positive and sound optimistic, talking to a two-pound infant hooked up to a machine. But in my heart, I had feared that day might never come. When Mike dipped Connor's toes into the cold water of Ponquogue Beach, my eyes filled with happy tears.

Mike and I were painfully aware that things could have gone the other way. The NICU was a place of hope and joy, but also of tragedy and heartbreak. We'd show up in the morning, and the baby whose crib had been next to Connor's for days or weeks would be gone. Early on, I'd ask where the baby went. I quickly learned not to ask.

And while it seemed like Connor suffered many complications, there were so many difficulties that he didn't face—and so many difficulties that he *doesn't* face. We saw it all during his almost three months in that hospital. We prayed for those babies and their families. We still do.

We were lucky. We tried not to take that for granted. Despite our challenges, we knew we were blessed. And we were thankful. We still are.

With things settling down at last, I finally felt comfortable drafting a family tree with Connor on it. I knew a lot about my side, but I needed to learn more about my in-laws. During a Sunday dinner at Mike's parents' house, they jotted down names and nationalities. Mike's ancestry was German, Irish, Scottish, Welsh, and Lithuanian.

"Wait a minute," I said, looking at the paper. "Where's the Italian?"

My question was met with confused looks. "What do you mean?"

"Grammy Eva is half Italian," I said.

Now they were looking at me like I was nuts—especially Eva.

"Grammy's not Italian," Erin said.

"Yes, she is," I said, suddenly unsure. "Erin, you said so the day I met you all. You said that's why she brought cannolis to dinner… because she's half Italian."

They all burst out laughing.

"I was joking!" Erin said. "I guess I didn't realize back then, that you weren't used to our family's sarcastic sense of humor. I was just teasing Grammy for bringing an Italian dessert to an Irish occasion."

"You mean all this time I thought Eva was half Italian, and Mike was an eighth Italian, and my *son* was one sixteenth Italian, all because of a joke?"

Now I was laughing too. It doesn't really change anything, but I'm big into heritage and family trees, and I had gone more than two years thinking there was some Italian in Mike's family. That awkward first St. Patrick's Day dessert was still providing amusement for all of us.

St. Patrick's Day dinner with Mike's family has been an annual tradition ever since that first meeting. And even though we all know the stories by heart, someone always mentions the store-bought cupcakes and the Italian cannolis. And we all laugh.

We took Connor to Mass with us every Sunday, even when he was attached to the monitor. When he was about a year old, we starting giving him money to put in the collection basket, instead of using an envelope. We wanted him to understand that we donate to the church.

But he was always a little confused when the basket was thrust in front of him. We had to prod him every week, "Put the money in the basket. No, don't take money out. Put the money in the basket."

We were out of town one weekend so we went to an unfamiliar church. As we walked up the steps, Connor asked, "Where are we going?"

We entered the narthex and Connor said loudly, "Oh, church! Amen, alleluia, put the money in the basket!"

That was one of several funny lines Connor had as a toddler. Once we were out to dinner with Mike's cousin Chris and his girlfriend. Little Connor was chatting up a storm with the girlfriend. Finally, Chris said, "What am I, chopped liver?"

I said, "Don't take it personally, Chris. Connor is all about the ladies."

A few minutes later, the waitress came over. Connor smiled at her and said, "Hi! I'm Connor. I'm all about the ladies."

Another time he was drawing with markers, and he suddenly jumped up and ran over to me dramatically. Seemingly crying but without any tears, he showed me his hands with bright red marks on them.

"I'm bleeding! I'm bleeding! Oh, the pain! It hurts!"

I examined his hands and said, "Um, Connor, that's red magic marker. See?"

I grabbed a wet wipe and rubbed it off.

"Oh! Never mind," he said cheerfully and went back to his drawing.

Once when he was about three, we had a bunch of people over around Christmas time. The song "I Saw Mommy Kissing Santa Claus" came on the radio. Suddenly the music stopped.

Everyone looked over to the stereo. Connor was standing in front of it, hands on his hips, with a disgusted look on his face. It was obvious he had turned it off.

"I don't like that song!" he exclaimed. The rest of us exchanged glances and struggled not to smile.

Of course, Mommy shouldn't be kissing anyone other than Daddy.

Despite what many people think, the city has plenty of things for kids to do. In the winter, the Museum of Natural History was like our second home, since it was just a few blocks from our apartment. Connor would wander the halls, talking gibberish to the life-sized dioramas of animals and skeletons of dinosaurs.

We also spent some winter days in the Gymboree play space, and we joined a program called *Music Together* in which families sing and play simple musical instruments with their kids in a big circle. Connor really loved music.

In warmer weather, we frequently took Connor to the playgrounds in Central Park and Riverside Park. He especially loved the fountains and sprinklers. He took his first unaided steps at the Central Park Zoo. And the Sheep Meadow was a great spot for Connor to practice walking and just lounge around on a blanket with us

Even just walking around the city was fun. We often bumped into people we knew—especially friends from the CRC, since we all lived in the vicinity of Holy Trinity. One day, I was walking with

Connor in his stroller, and we bumped into Dave Cervini, who had helped start the "Cool Roman Catholics" group years earlier.

I said, "Connor, this is Dave! If not for him, you wouldn't be here. He runs the group that brought Daddy and me together!"

Connor was too young to understand, but I looked up and Dave's eyes were a little red. He said, "Wow, that really means a lot."

It was true! It's amazing how one person's initiative can change so many lives.

We also frequented the Boat Basin Café and Pier 71—casual outdoor restaurants on the Hudson River. Both were kid- and dog-friendly, which was great for us since we had one of each. I googled the Boat Basin one day to double-check its hours, and I spotted a review that said, "Too many kids and dogs." It was then that I realized we had crossed over to the "married with kids" side.

By the time Connor was almost three, we were outgrowing our Manhattan apartment. They say the smaller the kid, the bigger the gear. It's so true. We ended up renting a storage unit. When that filled up, we discussed renting a second one. At that point, we felt it was time to move.

We loved Manhattan, but we also liked the idea of raising Connor in the suburbs. Plus, we wanted to be closer to both sets of parents, who wanted more time with their grandson. And it would be nice to park our car in the driveway instead of in a garage charging $500 a month.

So we sold our city apartment and bought a house in a cute neighborhood in Nassau County near a train to the city, where we both still worked. After purchasing the house, we gave Connor a tour while it was still empty. We brought him upstairs and showed him his bedroom. It was just four walls, a closet, and two windows. But I excitedly said, "This is your room, Connor! What do you think?"

He burst into tears—I mean serious sobs. Mike and I exchanged surprised looks.

I knelt down and hugged him and asked, "What's wrong, Connor?"

"There's no bed!!" he sputtered out.

I guess we didn't set that up properly for him.

Once we were on Long Island, it was easier to visit our families. Connor was blessed to spend time with two of his great-grand-mothers—Florence on my mom's side and Eva on Mike's mom's side. They both adored him. He would toddle around, plunking the keys on Grammy Florence's piano, or waving at Grammy Eva's reflection in the skylight over the table at Mike's parents' house. Florence and Eva have both since passed away, but Connor still remembers them fondly.

By the time Connor was three, he had been diagnosed with sensory processing disorder, ADHD, and other developmental delays. He also had asthma. It's very common for preemies to have neurolog-ical issues and respiratory conditions, since their nerves and lungs weren't done developing when they were born.

So we started him on a regimen of physical therapy (for "gross motor skills" like balance and walking), occupational therapy (for "fine motor skills" like using a crayon), and sensory therapy (so he wouldn't be overstimulated by sights and sounds).

If you're in the special needs world, you already know what all of that means, and if you're not, you probably don't want to hear about it. But suffice it to say, it was time-consuming and required dedication by Mike and me. I took him to lengthy therapy sessions multiple days each week, and we followed an intensive daily home program. Connor got tired of it, and so did we. But we were told his whole future depended on lessening his deficits during those early years when his body and brain were still developing, so we kept at it for many years.

We'll never know for sure if any of it helped, because we don't know what he would have been like had we *not* done those things, but Connor was a trooper, and he has come a very long way.

In elementary school, the teachers constantly told us how distractible he was in class, but they also noted that he was extremely intelligent, well-spoken, eager to please, and had a delightfully upbeat personality. He was given accommodations for his issues, but he also worked very hard and earned high grades throughout grammar school. We were so proud of him.

We tried putting him on medication for a brief time during grammar school to help him sit still and focus. The first medication we tried left him bouncing off the walls. We dropped that one after a day. The second med seemed to work a little for a year or so, but the side effect was that he was noticeably depressed toward the end of each day. We took him off that one too. His focusing didn't seem any worse once he was off the meds, and his mood definitely improved. That was the end of that experiment.

Connor had some trouble making friends at first. Social skills are another common challenge for former preemies. We put him in social skills groups, and over time, we were grateful that several children accepted him with his quirks, invited him to gatherings, and considered him a friend. We were also grateful to the parents of those kids because, let's face it, it's the parents who teach their children to be kind to others and accepting of differences.

Connor wasn't a great artist due to his fine-motor delays, but he still managed to produce "entertaining" artwork at school. Assigned to "draw a picture of one of your parents at work," Connor drew a horrifying image of a man with a giant needle in his hand, raised over a child on a table. The bubble over the child said, "No, no, please don't!"

We asked Connor what this represented and he said, "Oh, that's just Daddy giving a kid a shot."

I smiled but privately wondered if Mike would ever be allowed back in the school.

Connor was a "joiner." He wanted to be in every club at school. He joined his grammar school band, playing the baritone horn at first and then tuba. He had seen Mike play tuba at his college band reunion and decided it looked like a lot of fun. Connor eventually "made All County" which means he played in a special concert featuring the best musicians in our county.

Connor was also in the school's Ballroom Dance Club. Since Mike and I both enjoyed ballroom dance, we were fans of the show *Dancing with the Stars* and Connor got into it. He ended up winning multiple medals in his school's ballroom dance competitions.

In the Cub Scouts, he camped, tried archery, and learned all sorts of helpful skills. Mike, a former Scout, was the Cubmaster, so they enjoyed lots of father-son bonding. Connor even won first place for design in the Pinewood Derby miniature car contest one year. And he was one of several scouts from his pack who were in the color guard for the National Anthem on the field at Citi Field at the start of a Met game one year. It was something I never would've imagined during my summer days selling beer at Shea Stadium.

Connor joined his school's drama club and got good laughs playing the nerd "Harvey" in *Bye Bye Birdie*—the same show in which I had played "Ursula" in high school. It's funny how things come back around.

Connor also did Tae Kwon Do for a few years, working his way up to "candidate," the belt right before black belt.

We put Connor in a bunch of sports in his younger years so he could try them out. We quickly learned that he was not all that skilled at Little League, lacrosse, or soccer. He was on the swim team for a few years and did okay, but he didn't love it.

But the boy could run! Connor may not have had the coordination for sports involving bats or balls, but he had a ton of energy, so track became his thing. His asthma held him back at times, but he became a solid distance runner. He ran his first 5K race when he was seven. By the time he was 10, we were traveling with him to other states to compete in the Cross Country National Championships. Watching him cross the finish line of his first nationals, I choked up remembering his NICU doctors saying he would probably have lifelong respiratory issues, especially since he was on a ventilator. You need good lungs to run, not to mention for playing tuba.

But as proud as we were of Connor's lungs, we were even prouder of his "heart." Connor was a sweet kid. He was kind to others and empathetic if anyone was sad. In addition to several academic awards during elementary school, he received a "Character Award." That might've been the one that thrilled us the most.

Parenting is never easy, and you get bombarded with conflicting advice. Some of Connor's teachers thought we were too hard on him, given his challenges, while our parents thought we weren't demanding enough. We tried to strike a balance but I know there were times when we were either too tough or too soft.

We tried not to treat Connor like he was "different." Various experts gave assorted names to Connor's issues but we tried not to get hung up on labels. Connor was aware that he was considered "special needs" but we didn't let him use that as an excuse to give up. We believed he would succeed, so he believed it too.

So take heart, parents of preemies! It's a long road with many hills and valleys, and it often feels like you're taking one step forward, two steps back. And there are no guarantees. But for us and many of the other families who have been through this journey, there was health and happiness at the end of the road.

When I look back on the darkest days, I never forget the promise I made when Connor was being resuscitated in the hospital. I told God I would teach Connor to love Him. Mike and I raised Connor as a Catholic, took him to church, and told him about the many people who prayed for him. And we urged him to pray for others. He did, and he still does. So do we.

CHAPTER 11

The Notorious P.A.B.

"Happiness is not having what you want...It is wanting what you have."

–Rabbi Hyman Schachtel

My career took a backseat to my family once I got married and had Connor. During those first few years, there were many interruptions to my time at Fox News—my honeymoon, home bed rest early in my pregnancy, my hospitalization before and after Connor's birth, and maternity leave. I used up every saved vacation and comp day, as well as short-term disability during my bed rests. Fox was terrific about giving me all the time I needed.

When I finally returned, I had weekend hosting shifts and early weekday hours for a bit. To some, it looked like a demotion, but at that stage in my life, I didn't care what it looked like. Those hours were actually perfect for our family. Mike was working weekdays, so we only needed a nanny to cover a few hours on days when our hours overlapped. It was tag-team parenting, but we were glad Connor usually had at least one parent at home.

I did a lot of substitute hosting—frequently co-anchoring *America's Newsroom* with Bill Hemmer; *Happening Now* with Jon

Scott; and weekend shows with Gregg Jarrett, Kelly Wright, and Eric Shawn. I also did some cut-ins, Fox News Radio shifts, and voice-overs. It was "a little of this and a little of that," but it kept me busy five days a week.

Bouncing around was chaotic at times but also enjoyable. I got to work with many different on-air and off-air crews. I didn't have a show to call my own, or one specific group to bond with day after day, but I knew almost everyone at Fox News after a year as a "floater." And I had been renewed for a third three-year contract—still full-time with benefits—even after my extended absences, so I considered myself lucky.

In early 2007, a crazy new show debuted on Fox News in the middle of the night. It was called *Red Eye w/ Greg Gutfeld*, and it aired on weeknights at 3 AM Eastern Time (midnight on the west coast). This late-night talk show put a humorous twist on the news of the day. The host, Greg Gutfeld, had a sharp wit and, true to his name, the guts to tell it the way he saw it. He was joined every night by the hilarious Bill Schulz, referred to by Greg as "my grotesque sidekick," and by Andy Levy, a brilliant Columbia grad and Army vet dubbed the "ombudsman." These three characters were joined by two other guests every night—often comedians, actors, or Fox News personalities.

Red Eye was irreverent, to put it mildly. Loaded with bizarre jokes, biting satire, sexual innuendo, and bleeped profanities, it quickly earned harsh critics and a devoted cult following. I was in the latter category. I first caught *Red Eye* when I subbed on the overnight shift for a week while the usual anchor took a vacation. By the end of the week, I was hooked. Normally I struggled to stay awake during overnights, but not once *Red Eye* started airing. I would wait with eager anticipation for the clock to strike 3, and spend the next hour laughing until I spit out my Diet Coke.

Seemingly oblivious to the emergence of DVRs and YouTube, the panelists would say and do all kinds of outrageous things for a laugh, rationalizing that "it's the middle of the night. Nobody's watching!"

But people *were* watching. In fact, this middle-of-the-night show started to beat out many daytime cable shows in the ratings. Fan sites cropped up online—most notably "The Activity Pit," where loyal viewers would comment enthusiastically about the previous night's show and suggest funny intros and guests for the next night.

One day in the hallway, I bumped into Todd Kelly, a Fox producer I'd known for years who now worked on *Red Eye*. I told him I was a huge fan. He said, "Are you asking to be a guest?"

Actually, I wasn't. I didn't consider myself nearly funny enough to share a set with Greg, Bill, and Andy. But now that he mentioned it, that would be a blast!

"Are you asking me to be a guest?" I responded.

He said, "I think you'd be great! I'll talk to the guys."

Sure enough, I was invited on the show. I was also given a "heads up": "The women on this show don't wear suits. They wear sexy dresses and high heels."

I already knew that, being a fan of the show. But I was a woman in my 40s and the mom of a two-year-old who needed lots of attention. I felt tired and beaten up—like I'd left my "mojo" behind in that maternity ward hospital bed. I realized I would have to up my game to hold my own with the *Red Eye* gang.

The day of my first appearance, I was given the topics well in advance and spent hours reading through them and coming up with my best quips. I put on a flattering black dress and went down to the green room for the 8 PM taping.

I had never met Greg, Bill, or Andy before, and when I saw them for the first time, I felt like a total fan girl. It was ridiculous considering that I had met countless major celebrities by that time, and these guys were technically my co-workers. But I rambled on about how much I loved the show and hoped I could do it justice. They were welcoming, and the booker, Michaela Huntley, kindly assured me that I looked like a "hot mama" and that the notes I'd submitted were funny.

The show went well. Greg's opening monologue killed. Bill played his role of "token liberal" with his usual comic genius. "TV's Andy Levy" cracked everyone up with his fact-checking, which was mainly tongue-in-cheek since almost nothing that was said on *Red Eye* was meant to be taken seriously. Our fifth panelist, former CIA officer Mike Baker, was entertaining as always. And to my relief, my comments got laughs.

Although my jokes were tame compared to those of the others, they were completely different from anything I'd ever said on air before. I had been writing serious news for my entire career. For *Red Eye*, I was essentially writing comedy. It was out of my wheelhouse, and I felt uneasy delivering some of my lines.

But sometimes it's good to go outside your comfort zone. Now a wife and mother, I had let myself fade into the background and was putting all my attention on my husband and son. It was a happy, healthy role to an extent, but not ideal for an on-air personality. I had gotten too comfortable. *Red Eye* shook me out of my complacency.

Within months I was a "regular," appearing on the show every other week for almost two years. I shared the set with comedian Colin Quinn, actor Dean Cain, and so many other fun celebs. I immensely enjoyed the appearances and also going out after the taping—a *Red Eye* tradition for a while. Although I still generally followed my policy of keeping my work life separate from my social life, I couldn't resist hanging out on *Red Eye* nights. Since the tapings wrapped by 9:30 PM or so, the whole gang would head to the bar across the street for more laughs with whomever the guests were that night.

Even if I'd gone straight home after the tapings, Mike and Connor would already be in bed, so I wasn't sacrificing family time by going out. And the *Red Eye* folks were fun. Die-hard fans know some of the behind-the-scenes guys like Joshua McCarroll and Tommy O'Connor from their "cameos" during silly *Red Eye* skits. They were just as funny in person. And Michaela was always a good time.

Eventually, my buddy Bill Schulz created an alter ego for me: "The Notorious P.A.B." (a takeoff on the rapper "Notorious B.I.G."). Bill wrote sarcastic "disclaimers" for me to read at the start of the show, inspired by popular raps. They were clever, obnoxious, and completely over-the-top. To me, what made them so funny was the fact that they were totally out of character for me. I believe it was that incongruity that made people laugh.

My online popularity was soaring, especially with the younger demographic, and it was clearly due to *Red Eye*. The show often drew more than 400,000 viewers—big ratings for the middle of the night. Fans commented on how great it was to see me shed my buttoned-up daytime image and show my "edgy" side. A David Combs painting of me sitting on a throne reigning over the severed heads of Greg, Andy, and Bill was auctioned off on eBay for more than $500. I was even offered a large sum to appear on *Celebrity Wife Swap*. (I turned it down.)

Fox management took notice of the high ratings during my *Red Eye* appearances and started booking me more on various daytime shows. I was also encouraged to show my figure on *Red Eye* and given some revealing dresses to wear.

I think all the positive feedback went to my head. Looking back now, I regret some of my outfits and comments.

No longer feeling like a frumpy middle-aged woman, I started wearing shorter skirts and lower necklines for my *Red Eye* appearances. In my defense, many of my dresses looked more decent when I was standing in front of the full-length mirror in my office. They were a tad shorter than my usual but still respectable. But the bottom of a dress gets a lot shorter once you're *sitting* on the set. I ended up showing a lot of leg.

The same thing goes for tops. My dresses showed some cleavage but nothing outrageous when I stood at my mirror. But things changed on the set. When you sit, your top sometimes opens up a bit more (or a *lot* more). Add to that the fact that the cameras were often positioned high up and tilted down, so the angle I saw in my mirror was not the angle the viewers saw. A few times, I cringed when I saw the tape of the show.

Unfortunately, but not coincidentally, those are the shows and frame grabs that went viral online. A Google search of my name would turn up images of me in sexy outfits, labeled "Fox News Channel anchor," suggesting that this was how I dressed to deliver the news. It absolutely was not! My daytime wardrobe was conservative by Fox standards. Those *Red Eye* images of me, from a late-night talk show, made me look unprofessional. But the fact is I did wear those outfits, albeit in the middle of the night. I have to own it.

My jokes, too, were starting to push the limits of propriety. I got such a great reaction every time I said something mildly outrageous, it encouraged me to go even further the next time. Fans started creating video montages of my *Red Eye* appearances. Several of them went viral, racking up hundreds of thousands of views. I was psyched when one was featured by pop icons Olivia Munn and Kevin Pereira on their popular weekly cable show *Attack of the Show*.

But now I feel like I went too far at times. There's nothing to be done about it now, and the fact is I really loved those *Red Eye* days.

I had to cut back on my appearances once I got my next gig with Glenn Beck, but *Red Eye* continued until 2017, with Tom Shillue taking over as host when Greg became co-host of *The Five*. Greg also got his own Saturday night talk show, which was so successful that it was moved to weeknights in 2021. On August 17th of that year, after rising in the ratings for months, *Gutfeld!* reached 2.1 million viewers, beating every other late-night show including its nearest rival, Stephen Colbert's *Late Show*. Not bad for a guy who used to say, "I'm gonna be fired tomorrow!" pretty much every night when I worked with him.

In 2009, charismatic radio host Glenn Beck arrived at Fox News, and I was named the update anchor for his new daily 5 PM television show. The initial plan was for me to just do a short newscast in the middle of his hour. But Glenn typically kept me on the air to chat for a while after my updates. Since he was alone on the set, he liked having someone with whom he could interact. I usually played the "straight man," rolling my eyes while he cracked jokes.

I liked Glenn. He was a provocateur on air, as is the case with most radio personalities, but in person he was kind to everyone and well-liked. He was also sincere in his beliefs and truly cared about society as a whole. And despite his tendency to focus on gloom-and-doom predictions, he was funny and charming.

Glenn's show was an instant hit, drawing up to three million viewers every night at its peak. That was more than rivals CNN, MSNBC, and CNN Headline News *combined*. He and I had good chemistry, so at some point Fox added a live web show. Every night for a while, when Glenn's TV show ended at 6 PM, the two of us would move to the "dot-com" studio, where Glenn would ruminate for another half hour on whatever topics he felt warranted further discussion while I chimed in now and then.

Glenn's show on Fox lasted two and a half years. I was his update anchor for his entire run, and it was a pleasure getting to know him and his gang from Mercury Radio Arts. Mike, Connor, and I attended a pool party at Glenn and his wife Tania's home, and I have a collection of his bestselling books.

But the more popular Glenn became, the louder his detractors got. The left attacked him for sounding the alarm about the overreach of so-called "social justice warriors," among many other things. Moderates on the right found his conspiracy theories too extreme. His credibility on certain issues was called into question. And since he talked for hours every day, he occasionally put his foot in his mouth, and it was never overlooked. Advertisers started to bail, and Fox urged Glenn to tone it down, which he was unwilling to do since he considered his show a "movement."

So Glenn took his show to his own online platform, GBTV. His subscription-based internet program was very successful. It was later renamed The Blaze and was eventually aired by dozens of television carriers.

Looking back more than a decade later, a lot of the predictions Glenn made on his show have come true. Back then, people described him as "kooky" if they were polite, or "insane" if they were less charitable. I have to admit that as I sat through his show

Monday through Friday for more than two years, watching him scribble on his giant blackboard, I *hoped* he was crazy, because if he was right, our country was headed for big trouble.

Unfortunately, Glenn Beck turned out to be right about a whole lot of things.

Anyway, he still hosts his TV and radio shows, goes on tours, writes books, and does a lot for charity through his non-profit organizations, Mercury One and the Nazarene Fund. In 2021, his organizations reportedly led a humanitarian effort to evacuate refugees and persecuted Christians trying to flee Afghanistan after it was taken over by the Taliban. Glenn worked directly with Pakistan's Prime Minister Imran Khan to try to provide flights out of the country. And back in 2014, he reportedly arrived at the US border with Mexico with tractor trailers full of food and teddy bears for tens of thousands of undocumented minors who crossed into Texas without their parents. He said these children were "caught in political crossfire" and that "we must help…we must open our hearts."

So while critics say he tries to stoke hate for money, I disagree. Say what you will about his views, but I know Glenn has a good heart.

Not long after Glenn Beck's departure, a new early morning show was launched on Fox News. Called *Fox & Friends First*, it aired at 5 AM Eastern Time every weekday morning. After months of auditions, four co-hosts were officially named: Ainsley Earhardt, Heather Childers, Heather Nauert, and myself. For the following year and a half, the four of us rotated, two at a time, so each of us got to co-anchor with all of the others. I'd be paired with Ainsley for a week, then have a week "off," then be paired with Heather Nauert, then a week off, then a week with Heather Childers, and so on.

I was given a new "show host" contract. Although I had hosted more than a thousand hours at Fox already, many of them were as a sub so I was paid as a "cut-in anchor" for much of that time. Now that I was officially a host, I got a bump in pay.

Of course, I wasn't "off" during my off weeks from the 5 AM show. I hosted hour-long live web shows on FoxNews.com called *Strategy Room*, and I anchored cut-ins and breaking news on FNC and sometimes on The Fox Business Network, which had launched in 2007.

I enjoyed hosting the 5 AM show. It was a unique pleasure to co-anchor with women. Since I was usually paired with male co-anchors, I hadn't had the opportunity to get to know my female colleagues as well.

Now I worked with three women on a regular basis, which was refreshing. Ainsley is as bubbly off camera as she is on. Heather Nauert and I bonded over our sons, and Heather Childers and I became good friends.

I also had the privilege of becoming friends with our meteorologist, Janice Dean, who I admire for her role in the successful effort to unseat New York Governor Andrew Cuomo. It took courage. She could've stayed out of politics and just stuck with the weather. But when her husband Sean's mother and father both died of Covid in separate facilities that were forced by the state to take infected patients, she started speaking out. Ultimately, it was sexual harassment allegations that did Cuomo in, but Janice kept the heat on him, and I believe that helped turn the tide against him.

Obviously, the downside of anchoring a 5 AM show was waking up in the dead of night. I set my alarm for exactly 1:42 every morning. I had my routine down to the minute. 1:45 was too late, but if I got up at 1:40, I was waiting for my car service, and that was two more minutes of sleep I was missing!

The upside was that Fox provided a car for my trip in. The drive took less than 30 minutes at that hour. When I commuted by train, it took more than an hour door to door. At least with smartphones I could "read in" while sitting on the train, provided I got a seat. But it was much easier to prep in the back of a car.

Once I got to work, preparing for the 5 AM show was a race against time. For other shows, I allowed four hours to prep, but I cut it much closer for *Fox & Friends First*. The show was only an hour long, and there were only a few guest segments. Despite its name, our show had very little in common with the show it preceded, *Fox & Friends*. Our show was more of a straight news roundup, with a high story count and very little time for on-air chit-chat.

Our excellent stage manager, Matt Rodriguez, kept us on our toes. (Yes, we called them "stage managers," and it's an apt description since our shows were like Broadway productions, except without rehearsals.) I can't say enough about how fantastic the stage crews were at Fox News Channel. And their jobs weren't easy.

Fox didn't believe in plopping anchors in chairs and leaving them there for an hour. The studio camera operators couldn't simply set their focus at the start of the show and then snooze for the rest of the hour. We were always "on the move." We would stand for one block, sit for the next, then hop over to the guest set for the next. We showed off every corner of our studios, including walls which were basically giant screens with changing digital graphics. It was all about movement and color to hold the viewers' attention in the age of short attention spans.

There was a lot of zooming and panning on Fox News. And guests were coming and going, needing to be seated and mic'ed. The directors and control room crews had to adapt to frequent breaking news, when we would "rip the rundown": abandon our previous plan and ad lib through the entire hour, bringing in last-minute phone interviews and live FaceTimes. The prompter operators had an especially nerve-wracking job, since the anchors liked to go off script. Plus our digital scripts were sometimes updated by writers or producers while the anchors were literally reading them live on air.

The Fox News crews handled everything that was thrown at them, and they also managed to have fun with each other and with the anchors during commercial breaks. I have so many fond memories of chatting with stage managers Erin Horstmann and Joel Fulton, among many others. The behind-the-scenes folks at Fox were top-notch at their jobs, and great people besides.

During my year-and-a-half as 5 AM anchor, since I was usually standing beside a female co-anchor, the viewers noticed something about me that most had never realized before: I'm somewhat short. Not surprisingly, I was shorter than all my male co-anchors, but that never struck anyone as odd. But my female co-anchors towered over me.

I'm five-foot-two and three-quarter inches, to be exact. I had never considered myself particularly short, but comments were being posted, and our producers suggested that I wear higher heels. I pointed out that I was already wearing four-inch heels, but so were my co-anchors.

"So wear five inch heels," I was told.

I wasn't sure why it was necessary to hide the fact that I was short. It's not a crime. But I dutifully went shopping for five-inch heels. They were not compatible with my personal style, and they were incredibly uncomfortable. I could not walk in them at all. So every morning I wore ballet slippers to the studio and pulled my high heels out of my bag at the last minute, once I was seated on set. But the extra inch wasn't enough, especially since my co-anchors sometimes wore five-inch heels, too. So I was also given a box to balance on during standing two-shots.

One day my stilettos ended up causing me pain, humiliation, and a good laugh.

Each day toward the end of our show, we'd do a tease for the upcoming *Fox & Friends*. On Friday mornings over the summer, there was always a concert in our plaza, so we usually promoted the upcoming recording artist.

On this day, Heather Childers announced that Pat Benatar would be performing. *Pat Benatar*…whose songs I sang when I was lead singer in a basement band during high school. *Pat Benatar*… whose songs I sang to my son when he was clinging to life in the neonatal ICU. *Pat Benatar*…my musical idol for my entire life… was in our plaza!

People in my business generally play it cool around celebrities and don't fawn over them or hassle them for selfies or autographs. But there are exceptions. I told Heather I was going to rush out of the studio the second our show ended so I could catch Pat before she started performing. She said, "You go girl!"

There was very little time. I knew I had to catch her during the commercial break and the *Fox & Friends* intro. I decided not to waste time changing out of my pumps. Dumb decision. I sprinted to the elevator, emerged on the first floor, and asked the security guards to let me out the side entrance behind the stage. They obliged.

Pat was just finishing a warm-up song onstage. She was stepping down, just a few yards away from me! This was my chance. I ran. It had been raining. The plaza had a smooth surface that was *very* slippery when wet. One of my spike heels slipped as I ran, and I knew in a second, "Oh, no, I'm going down…all the way down."

As I was hurtling to the ground, I grabbed a temporary metal barrier, foolishly thinking it would hold me, but those things are not at all sturdy. The barrier toppled over with a loud clatter, and I fell on top of it, my ribs hitting the metal bars hard. I let out an involuntary yelp which drew everyone's attention, not that anyone could've missed this scene.

"Anchor down! Anchor down!" one of the security guards comically announced into his walkie-talkie.

Luckily this happened behind the stage so only a handful of people saw my fall, but Pat was one of them. As I struggled to stand back up, she scurried over and said, "Oh, my gosh! Are you ok?"

"I'm fine," I said, although my ribs really hurt, and then I blurted out, "I love you! I sang your songs to my son when he was in the hospital. I sang your songs when I was in a band. I have all your albums. I've been to your concerts. I just wanted to meet you."

"Thank you! That's so…" she started to say, then… "Oh my, you're bleeding."

Yup, the palms of my hands, and both knees, were bleeding. Pat helped me dab at my wounds with a tissue.

This had played out differently in my mind.

The security guards were anxious to hustle me inside so I could be tended to, but I wasn't leaving without a photo. Not after all that!

I asked Pat if she'd indulge me for another minute. She was so kind—exactly the way I knew she'd be. She was also as beautiful as ever. She said, "Of course! Take your time."

We ducked into the building, and one of the guards snapped the shot. I thanked Pat and the guard profusely. I'd do it all again to get that photo with my idol and the chance to thank her for being such an inspiration.

Aside from some cuts and bruises, I was fine after the fall, but it was a "workplace accident," so I had to fill out paperwork and all that. And I got a call from Roger Ailes asking if I was okay. Apparently, bad news and embarrassing falls travel fast.

I'm often asked about Roger. He was the CEO of Fox News Channel starting from its inception in 1996. He resigned in 2016 amid allegations of sexual harassment by anchors and other Fox employees. He died less than a year later at age 77.

I was very fond of Roger. To me, he was like a wise, funny old uncle. We met in his office a few times a year, and he gave me great advice. He was a straight shooter—something very rare in these times. He would tell me honestly what he believed my shortcomings were on the air and off, and coach me on how to overcome them. And he did it with a sense of humor. Roger liked to make people laugh.

One day, I wore a pantsuit on air. Later, in my office, my phone rang.

"Mr. Ailes is on the line for you."

"Okay, thanks."

I waited and heard Roger pick up a second later.

"Nice pantsuit, Hillary!"

I laughed heartily and said, "Message received. No more pantsuits."

He said, "Thanks, gotta go! Have a good one."

That brief exchange was one of many that made me chuckle. He came up with a lighthearted way to make his minor point, instead of delivering his "pantsuit edict" in a stern tone. Roger was funny. I liked that.

Some of my friends thought I should be offended that my boss was requiring me to wear skirts on air. But this was the TV business. I felt that management had the right to specify a dress code within reason. Plus, Fox gave me a wardrobe allowance of thousands of dollars per year. That money was controlled by a wardrobe consultant. She and her assistants would hand me outfits to try on, evaluate them while I stood at the mirror, and then purchase the ones they liked, with my input. To me, since Fox paid for my clothes, that made it like a "uniform." I had to wear a uniform when I worked at McDonald's, and I got paid a whole lot less (and it was ugly).

Roger and I would also chat about our personal lives. He loved his wife and son. He talked about them all the time, in glowing terms. After I got married and had Connor, we would talk about our worries over having an "only child," and our concerns about not being home enough for our sons. Mike, Connor, and I went to Yankee games with Roger and his family in his box, and to a summer party at his home.

Did Roger sometimes say inappropriate things? Unfortunately, yes, as did many other men from his generation with whom I worked over the years. While the rest of us at Fox took mandatory sexual harassment seminars every other year, Roger seemed unaware that the times had changed. But in my case, if he tried to steer the conversation in a bad direction, I'd say, "Cut it out, Roger," and he would. We'd go back to talking about Fox or about our families.

He did ask me to "twirl" whenever I first entered his office. This is something many other anchors have mentioned, and yes, it made me uncomfortable. I told myself it was maybe, sort of, possibly understandable because I was on television, after all. Still, I didn't like it. But it was a quick thing. He'd say, "You look good! You're taking care of yourself." And then we'd sit in chairs on opposite sides of the coffee table and talk.

Roger never hit on me. He never propositioned me. He never offered me promotions in exchange for sexual favors, and he never threatened to punish me for not sleeping with him. He never made a pass at me at all. If he got flirtatious, I shut him down, and he accepted it and moved on.

So I was stunned to hear the accusations made by some colleagues. At first, I had trouble believing them. I absolutely believed he made suggestive comments. But the stuff I was hearing about quid pro quos and bullying just didn't sound like the man I knew and admired.

However, after many months passing and after many women coming forward, some of whom I greatly respect, I had to gradually confront the possibility that Roger had a side I didn't know about.

This honestly broke my heart. Roger was good to me all those years. He kept me on, after all my time off. He stuck by me and gave me bits of advice that still help me to this day. His door was always open to me, and he never asked for anything in return. It hurts to think he wasn't the man I thought he was.

It's been many years now, and I'm still sad and confused by it all. I've talked to other women who feel the same way. Roger built something good. Fox News isn't perfect, but it's a much-needed alternative to the other mainstream news sources, which clearly lean left. Almost no one thought Fox News Channel would make it. But Roger had the skills and determination to turn a fledgling network into a media powerhouse. If only that were his legacy. Instead, due to his human weakness, he died a broken man.

CHAPTER 12

Patrick

Colleen was distraught when she called me one day back in the late 1980s.

"I'm pregnant," my twin sister choked out through tears.

This was not a happy development at that stage in her life. When her cycle went off schedule, she wasn't concerned at first, but eventually her doctor did a pregnancy test. She was stunned. Apparently, the warning that condoms are not 100 percent effective is true.

When she left the doctor's office, she briefly considered running in front of a truck that was passing on the street. Oddly, what stopped her was the thought, "No, that would hurt the baby I'm carrying."

She told me on the phone that she had considered abortion, but she was surprised to realize she already valued the life inside her, no matter how inconvenient it was.

But what would she do? She was young, unmarried, and didn't feel that she could give her child the life that he or she deserved. She had known the father for months, and their dates had seemed promising for a solid relationship. But the pregnancy news scared him off. She was on her own.

And the more immediate question was: How would she tell our parents? Colleen had always made our mom and dad proud. The thought of disappointing them was almost unbearable. It's the dread of having this one difficult conversation that leads many young women to make a different decision. But Colleen, with my support and that of our younger sister, Mary Lou, summoned her courage, buried her shame, and called our mom.

Mom was definitely shocked, but she quickly pivoted off her own dismay and assured Colleen that we would get through this together, as a family. Her unconditional love gave immense comfort to Colleen. To all of us, honestly. A mother's love is a powerful force.

But we knew the tougher conversation was still to come. My mom decided she should be the one to break the news to our dad. We expected this conversation to go very badly. My sisters and I knew when the bomb was going to be dropped, and we waited anxiously for word. My phone finally rang. My mom was in tears. My heart sank.

"I married a good man," she managed to say.

What? Maybe this won't be as bad as I thought.

"I can't stay on," she continued. "We already talked to Colleen. Dad and I are heading to see her. When I told him the situation, he wasn't angry. He was just upset *for her*. He said, 'Our daughter needs us there with her, as soon as possible. We have to go hug her.'"

Yes, my dad is a very good man. In that moment, he didn't judge Colleen. He knew that wasn't what was needed. She needed love. The role of protector doesn't end when your kids grow up. It just changes, from shielding them from wasps to supporting them in a life crisis.

But teens and young adults don't always comprehend this. It's easy to recognize that your parents love you when you make them proud. It's harder when you let them down. However, pride and love are two different things. Parents can be disappointed in their kids but still love them. I'm ashamed to say we underestimated our parents. I guess we sort of thought they loved us because we were generally good. No. They loved us. Full stop.

Of course, my parents would have preferred that Colleen had avoided this situation. But they were very proud of the choices she made afterwards, and they let her know they would be there for her. Without that support, this could've been a very different chapter.

With the consent of the baby's father, Colleen decided to place her child for adoption. It was a very difficult decision, and it wasn't for her own benefit. She would have raised her child had she believed it would be best for the baby. However, at the stage she was in, she felt that she could not give her child the best life possible. She knew there were young single moms who were wonderful parents who raised great kids. But she wanted her baby to have an upbringing similar to her own happy childhood, which was anchored by two loving parents.

Colleen quickly became attached to the baby. At one point, she had unexplained bleeding. (I guess it runs in our family.) She called me from the hospital crying, begging me to pray that the baby was okay. It turned out to be a false alarm. She later told me how surprised she was by her reaction. This was an unplanned and, at first, unwelcome pregnancy. She knew she wasn't even going to raise this baby, but she was desperate to keep her child alive and healthy. The maternal instinct is strong.

When Colleen started to show, friendly strangers would chat with her about her pregnancy. When she told them her baby would be adopted, she was surprised by how many of them knew prospective parents looking to adopt.

The person's eyes would widen, and they would launch into a hopeful pitch about an amazing couple who would be the perfect parents. They would scribble a name and number on any scrap of paper they could find and beg Colleen to call their cousin, dog-walker, and so on. Colleen soon had a collection of numbers from people who were probably praying daily that the pregnant lady from the library or store might call. It quickly became clear to her that there are no unwanted babies—just unplanned ones.

But Colleen stuck with her plan to work with an agency she was referred to by Birthright. Birthright is a great organization. It is non-political. Its mission is simply to support pregnant women who choose to carry their babies to term, whether they plan to raise them themselves or place them for adoption. Birthright refers pregnant women to counseling and other services, and even offers maternity clothes if needed. If the woman wants to keep her pregnancy a secret, Birthright will even set her up with an agency in another state who will place her with a supportive "host family" for the duration of the pregnancy.

Colleen gave her agency her parameters for the type of adoptive parents she wanted to raise her child. And they provided her with a packet of letters from anonymous prospective parents. She read through them carefully and forwarded her favorites to our mom, Mary Lou, and me.

It was striking to me how many loving couples were yearning to welcome babies into their homes. I got emotional reading their stories and feeling how deeply they ached to share their lives with a baby. One letter candidly opened with the observation that, "This is an almost overwhelming task to sit and write a profile. This is so extremely important to both of us." So true.

Many letters thanked Colleen for her "unselfish gift." They described beautiful nurseries and playrooms that were collecting dust as the husband and wife prayed for a baby. At one point, Colleen commented to me that she almost regretted having only one child to give. If only there were more to fill the empty arms of these loving couples.

I had heard the argument that a young unmarried woman should terminate her pregnancy because she might not be equipped to raise a child on her own. But reading these letters reinforced the fact that keeping the baby is not the only other option. There are so many couples who are unable to have a child of their own, who are longing to adopt. I wish more people would consider the adoption option.

Colleen chose a wonderful adoptive couple. They wrote:

"We have no doubt of our ability to give our unconditional love to your child…Your child will always know how he or she came to be a part of our family and have a healthy self-image and positive feelings about his or her birth parents…All of us intertwined in this act of love must respect and love each other always."

Colleen was not given the couple's name, but she spoke with them on the phone while she was pregnant. They were nervous, but Colleen tried to make conversation. She mentioned that she loved the beach and asked if they did too. They said yes and Colleen said, "Great! Next time you're there, bring the baby."

There was silence on the line. Colleen thought her phone had gone dead. "Hello?"

They both responded in emotion-filled voices, "Yes, we will."

Colleen realized they were crying.

They thanked her for choosing life. Colleen was glad she did.

Colleen gave birth to a very large and healthy boy. My parents were by her side, and my mom took a few cherished photos of the newborn in Colleen's arms.

I got a happy call saying, "It's a boy!"

My dad proudly described how strong the baby looked.

"There were football coaches at the nursery fighting to recruit him for their teams!" he joked.

It was bittersweet, of course, knowing we would never hold this baby or watch him grow up, but we were still bursting with joy at the news. My parents' first grandchild. My first nephew. Healthy and headed off to a great life in the Southeast.

Then came the heart-wrenching moment when the social worker arrived to carry this precious child out of our lives and into the loving arms of his adoptive parents. When our mom held her grandson for the last time, she struggled not to cry as she looked into his eyes and promised him, "*I will never, ever forget you.*"

Colleen gave the social worker a basket containing a letter telling her son how much she loved him, a stuffed bear, a pocket watch, and an audiotape of her singing to him. There were lots of tears.

The agency told Colleen the adoptive parents had given her son an Irish name. They were not Irish, but they knew she was, so they graciously chose a name that would honor her. It was a touching and comforting sign.

As time passed, Colleen was able to move on with her life joyfully. Although she never forgot her son, she had no regrets and was at peace with herself and her decisions. The rest of us were also happy, and our family bond was stronger than ever with the knowledge that we had weathered a crisis together and done what was best for this precious boy.

The arrangement was that Colleen would get one photo from the adoptive parents (through the agency) when her son turned three. After that, no updates were promised. She got the photo and gave me a copy, which I kept hidden in my wallet for decades. I stared at that photo until I had it memorized, then stared at it some more. I prayed that wherever he was, my nephew was happy and loved.

Years went by, then decades. Colleen married and had two beautiful daughters. She told her husband about her son before they married, and he accepted it with understanding and love. She didn't tell her daughters but planned to do so when they were older.

When Colleen's son turned 18, she was able to sign up for a registry that unites birth parents with their children if both parties are registered. Once Colleen registered, we all waited for a call that didn't come. His 19th birthday came and went, then his 20th, and 21st…. By his mid-20s, I began to realize we might never hear from him. This hurt, especially on his birthdays, but we comforted ourselves with the thought that he was with a loving adoptive family and hopefully thriving. Meanwhile, we took joy in our own expanding families.

We knew her son was now an adult, out of college, maybe married, maybe even a father himself. Every year on his birthday, my mom added "Baby Browne" to a church's prayer requests. I always hoped we would hear from the boy we never stopped praying for. But that hope was growing dim.

One December, Colleen and I were at a Christmas concert at Carnegie Hall featuring my old pal, Irish singer Andy Cooney (it became an annual event). We were in a festive, holiday mood when the Hibernian Festival Singers opened for the New York Tenors by singing a stirring rendition of "I Believe."

Suddenly Colleen was in tears. The song was beautiful, but this seemed extreme. During a break, we scurried to the ladies' room. Colleen told me she had listened to that song and sung it through-out her pregnancy to keep her spirits up. She even sang it on the cassette tape she recorded for her son and left in his basket. She had buried that memory for decades, hidden away with her own copy of the tape. Now it was all coming back.

Her desire to know what had become of him was intensified. I assured her that it was a good thing that he didn't feel inclined to search for his birth mother. It probably meant he was happy and fulfilled and didn't feel like anything was missing from his life.

"We might never know that for sure," she replied.

Perhaps inspired by the song, I responded, "You will know! You will know for sure that he is fine. I still believe that. You must believe it too."

In the back of my mind, I wasn't at all sure he would find us, but if he didn't, I was considering finding him, just to make sure he was okay. I didn't want to contact him, especially if he didn't want to be found. I just wanted word back: Is he healthy? Is he happy? That's all we wanted. That would've been enough.

I knew a couple who had hired a private investigator to find their long-lost child. It was a success. I was thinking maybe I would ask them for the PI's name and hire him to find my nephew. But

I wasn't ready to do anything like that. I still hoped he would find us first.

On an ordinary summer day almost three decades after her son's birth, Colleen's phone rang.

"Hi, this is Mary from the International Soundex Reunion Registry. We have a man looking for his birth mother, and your information is a match. Did you want to speak with him?"

And suddenly, that ordinary day turned into one of the happiest of her life.

His name was Patrick, and he lived in North Carolina. Colleen didn't know whether Patrick just wanted to speak with her on the phone for a few minutes, or if he was willing to meet her. Maybe he just wanted some medical information.

"Is he sick?" she asked Mary. "Does he need an organ donation? I'll give him anything he needs!"

"No," Mary replied. "It's nothing like that! He's getting married, and he wanted to tell you himself."

A short time later, the phone rang again, and for the first time since she heard his coos and cries in the hospital, Colleen again heard the voice of her son.

The first thing she said was, "I love you, I've always loved you, and I'll never stop loving you, and I hope you never doubted that."

Patrick assured her that he knew. His parents had always told him so, and it was reinforced by the letter Colleen left in his basket and the note she left with the adoption agency saying she hoped to meet him some day. He also assured her that his parents truly loved him as their own, and that he loved them back. This was music to Colleen's ears, and all of us were thrilled to hear it.

They talked on the phone for hours. He's a lawyer, just like Colleen. They love some of the same books. He thought about her often through the years, and was always grateful that she chose to give him life. He tried to find her when he was 18, with the help of his mom, but the agency sent him away. It turns out adoptees in North Carolina have to be 21 to check the registry—something we wish we had known at the time.

By the time Patrick turned 21, he was busy at college and the fear of what he may discover prevented him from searching. Years passed. He met a terrific woman at law school, and they were engaged. Because he was getting married and was happier than ever, he knew now was the time to search for and thank the woman who gave him life. His amazing fiancée, Stephanie, urged him to go ahead and find his birth mother. After several requests to the agency, he was referred to the registry and here they were!

Colleen and her husband, Mike, were over the moon! With some trepidation, they sat their teenaged daughters down and told them the story. My nieces were thrilled to learn they had a half-brother. Patrick had asked Colleen to let him speak with them as soon as they were told. On the phone, he told both of his half-sisters individually that he always wanted to be a big brother, and this provided him that opportunity.

Our family rejoiced and cried. Patrick e-mailed us some photos, and we could definitely see the resemblance. A few weeks later, we viewed his wedding on a livestream. As we watched, we pondered the fact that none of those people gathered in that church would be there if Colleen had made a different choice. And when Patrick and Stephanie start a family of their own, their kids will be alive because Colleen gave life to Patrick. It reminded me of my favorite movie, *It's a Wonderful Life*. One life has a ripple effect on so many others.

We felt overwhelming gratitude toward Patrick's parents, who lovingly raised him to become a caring young man. In the wedding video, it's clear that his mother and father are incredibly proud of the good man he has become.

Patrick and his lovely wife, Stephanie, came to New York a few months after the phone call for a joyful reunion with our family. Colleen picked them up at the airport. Recognizing Patrick from the photos and the wedding video, she ran and hugged him, and it was a cinematic-style airport scene.

Colleen drove Patrick and Stephanie to her home to meet her husband and daughters. They hit it off. Entering the dining room for the first time, Patrick was touched to see the centerpiece. It was his original blue hospital bracelet, which Colleen had saved all those years, mounted and surrounded by a bouquet of blue flowers.

Patrick and Stephanie stayed with Colleen and her family for several days. Colleen gave him a lengthy tutorial on our family tree and a tour of some special places from her past. Patrick, Stephanie, and Colleen's two daughters went to a local "escape room." They functioned really well as a team and came back to the house laughing about stories of their escape. They all made a shepherd's pie together, and Patrick and Stephanie demonstrated the dance they had learned for their wedding reception. It was surreal and magical.

Then it was time for him to meet the rest of us! We all gathered at my parents' home for a brunch that ended up lasting all day. I finally got to meet the man from the frayed, faded toddler photo in my wallet. We laughed and talked, and by the end of the day, it felt like we'd known him forever.

At one point, Patrick raised his mimosa glass and announced that he had prepared some remarks. He went on to read a lengthy, beautiful toast to our family, which included personal references to each of us. My husband, having endured countless sappy and funny Browne family "toasts and roasts" over the years, declared, "Yup, he's a Browne!"

It evolved into a "game night" in which we played a game similar to Charades called "Heads Up" on a phone app. One of the names to be guessed was a celebrity with the same last name as my grandmother. Recognizing the name from Colleen's family tree lesson, Patrick blurted out the clue, "Great Grandma's maiden name!"

Jaws dropped (maybe even some champagne glasses). This guy was good. Seriously, Patrick and Stephanie are phenomenal people. Patrick recently joined the board of a non-profit dedicated to serving adoptive parents and adoptees, with the hope of paying it forward and sharing his positive story. And Stephanie has done work for the Innocence Project. They will be wonderful parents one day, and God willing, their kids will have kids…all because of a choice Colleen made more than 30 years ago.

It's been years now since our family was made whole. Patrick and Stephanie visit our family up north at least once a year. We have so much fun with them!

One year, we all spent a long, special Memorial Day weekend together at my parents' home in the Hamptons. This had been a family tradition for years. My sisters and I and our families would drop everything to crowd into my parents' home to celebrate the start of summer together. It had gotten more difficult as our kids got older. Summer jobs, sporting events, and life in general had made it harder for all of us to get out east. But that year, we all made it happen.

It was the first time we could all be together with Patrick and Stephanie for an extended amount of time. We did all our favorite activities—boating, barbecuing, and singing karaoke on the deck. (In another sign that Patrick is truly a "Browne," he has never met a microphone he didn't like.)

The initial awkwardness faded. We reached a new level of comfort and familiarity and truly became one bigger and better family. We took a cherished family portrait that included Patrick and Stephanie.

Patrick brings out the best in each of us. We've always been a close family, but the addition of Patrick and Stephanie has made us even stronger and more appreciative of what we have.

Colleen and her family went down to North Carolina to visit Patrick and his wife in their new house. When they arrived, Patrick gave them a tour, and the centerpiece on their dining room table caught Colleen's eye. It was the basket Colleen lovingly prepared for him before his birth and gave the social worker to give to him when he was older.

My parents have also visited Patrick and Stephanie down south. Colleen's husband, who happily welcomed them into his family, even visited them on his own when a business trip took him to North Carolina. Mike, Connor, and I were planning a visit when Covid-19 ruined all plans. The visit is now planned for 2022.

And we all stay in touch. Colleen and Patrick speak on the phone regularly. Patrick and his wife get along great with Colleen's daughters. They have an active texting group going. My husband and I adore our nephew and his wife. Connor is thrilled to have another cousin. My parents are overjoyed to know their oldest grandchild. Mary Lou and her family are thrilled as well.

One of Mary Lou's daughters wrote a heartfelt essay about Colleen and Patrick on her college application. In it, she said, "*I admire my aunt so much for the decision she made.... People like my aunt and my cousin are living, breathing examples that there is a better option, one that values human life.*"

Patrick's mom asked him to arrange a phone call between her and Colleen. Her first words to Colleen were, "Thank you for having Patrick."

Colleen shared the news with friends and family, and told the story in her family's Christmas card. Many friends were moved to tears. One said, "What a beautiful ending!" Then paused and said, "No, what a beautiful beginning."

Being a proud big brother, Patrick flew up with his wife for his half-sister's high school graduation. But my niece was only given enough tickets for her parents and sister.

Turns out, a classmate had put out the word that he had two tickets he couldn't use, and he'd give them to whoever had the most compelling reason for wanting them. When my niece contacted him, he said he already had a taker but invited her to tell her "sob story" to try to change his mind. She did, and he said, "We can stop right there. The tickets are yours."

When my parents bought their house on eastern Long Island, my mom purchased a beach painting for the den. She had just one granddaughter at the time. The painting showed four girls playing on the sand with a younger boy. Over the years, my parents had three more granddaughters and then my son. They started calling the painting "The Prophecy" because each addition to our family matched a child in the painting.

Years ago, they related this story while showing the painting to a friend. The friend replied, "But what about the older boy?"

My parents, confused, were caught off guard and said nothing.

The friend pointed to the image of an older boy in the water, swimming away from shore. My stunned mom felt chills running down her spine.

"Oh!" she replied. "We never noticed that older boy."

Now that Patrick is a part of our lives, our cousin Patti McLaughlin has suggested that my mom, a painter herself, should repaint that older boy…swimming back to the rest of the family.

CHAPTER 13

Seasons

"*I*s there someplace safe you can go with your family?"
The Fox News security consultant, a retired NYPD cop, wanted me out of town ASAP. My latest stalker had landed at JFK Airport and was heading my way.

We knew this was coming. This psycho fan had been sending me disturbing emails for months. I should note that I never once responded to this guy. My reliable gut had signaled to me that this one might be trouble, so I never wrote back, from day one. His "relationship" with me was completely in his head.

But to him, it was real. He tracked down one of my sisters, my brother-in-law, and even one of my nieces, sending them e-mails and Facebook messages explaining that we were meant to be together and asking them to urge me to respond to him.

It ramped up after he read some false garbage online about me possibly getting a divorce. He emailed to say he was coming to take me away.

"Don't worry about your son," he assured me. "I will raise him like he's my own."

I showed the emails to Fox Security, who at first thought it was just talk.

But then he sent me his flight information and asked me to pick him up at the airport.

The police and FBI were looped in, and they confirmed that the man was in New York City and had stopped by the News Corp building, where he was not let in.

I was at home with Connor. Mike was at work.

"I can take Connor to my parents' house out east," I told the security guy. "But Mike's working today and for the next few days. He won't commute from out there."

"We'll put 24/7 bodyguards on you and your family out east," the consultant said, "and a separate detail on your husband."

I quickly packed, and Connor and I hit the road.

Out east, we contacted the local police as directed, to fill them in on what was happening. Mike, meanwhile, informed the police department in our hometown.

As Fox had promised, a bodyguard arrived at my parents' house and told us he would take an eight-hour shift, another guard would take the next eight hours, and another the next. I was grateful to Fox for having my back.

I was also glad that I had been careful not to share my whereabouts online. The stalker kept emailing me, asking why I didn't meet him at the airport and where I lived. He only knew my county and said he was heading there.

Afraid he might somehow find us at my parents' home, and trying to keep things light for Connor, we went to a street fair nearby. We strolled around the fairway eating cotton candy: Connor, his grandma and granddad, me—and a bodyguard scanning the crowd for a face matching the photo I had given him. (Since the stalker didn't consider himself a stalker, but rather a close friend and "rescuer," he had proudly emailed me a photo of himself.)

It was surreal and somewhat comical. Connor and I rode the carousel, and every time we came around to the bottom, we saw the guard leaning against the fence, watching us like a hawk.

Meanwhile, I got a text from my next-door neighbor, Claire, saying there was a man sitting outside my house, staring at it. For a split second, I thought it was the stalker. Then I realized it was Mike's bodyguard. I let Claire know what was happening. Needless to say, it was unsettling.

Thankfully, the night was uneventful, and the next day the third bodyguard arrived for his shift. As we sat in my parents' living room, Mike called to see how we were doing. I told him we were fine. He said he was very stressed and wanted to go for a bike ride.

"What about the bodyguard?" I asked.

"I'll tell him to take a break. There's no way for him to stay with me. Besides, there's no sign of the stalker."

"Okay, have fun," I said.

About an hour later he called again. Seeing his name on the phone, I picked up and cheerfully said, "We're still fine!"

Then I heard the sirens.

"Well I'm not fine! I'm in an ambulance. A car hit me and left me for dead in the middle of the road. I was thrown off my bike and hit the pavement head first. My helmet saved my life."

He texted me a photo of his face. I felt sick. The skin was missing from the entire left side of his face. It was just blood and flesh.

He said the car that hit him kept on driving. Other drivers parked where they were and ran over to him, lying in the middle of the road.

When the police came, they asked if anyone got a license plate number, and everyone said no.

"We thought this guy was dead! He was our priority."

Mike was checked over at the hospital. He was horribly banged up, bruised, and bloody, but miraculously no bones were broken, and he had no concussion. Unfortunately, he had lots of "soft tissue" and nerve damage. He had been riding fast since he had the right of way, so his fall was like being thrown against a brick wall at full speed. He still suffers from nerve damage and joint pain, and he has a large but faint patch of white-colored scarring on his left cheek from the road burn.

Was it the stalker? Probably not, but we'll never know. The cops didn't track him down until the next day, when the airport confirmed that he had left New York.

After that, the FBI banned him from flying into any New York airports, since he's not a US citizen. But a few months later, he tried to come back. He emailed me, saying the cops had told him to stay away from me. But he said he knew the police must be lying about my not wanting to see him. So he booked a flight to New York and went to his airport, but this time he was stopped before boarding. What a relief.

That was several years ago, and I'm only now starting to think he has probably given up. The dented helmet from Mike's accident is displayed in our living room as a reminder that life is short, and the time to set your priorities is now.

In addition to this guy and the police lieutenant from my News 12 days, I've had several other problematic fans over the years. It's not uncommon for celebrities to have stalkers, but it always surprised me because I'm not exactly a household name. All it takes is one obsessive fan to latch onto you.

One guy waited for me outside the News Corp building and followed me onto the uptown subway. I didn't know he was doing this until I got an email the next day asking, "How was that burger you took out from XYZ Diner?"

That day when I left work, I looked at everyone's face outside my building and checked to see if anyone was following me when I walked to the subway. I didn't see anyone suspicious that day. But a few days later I got another email from the same guy, indicating he had again followed me all the way home. It happened a couple more times.

I reported it to Fox Security, who reported it to the NYPD. They tracked down the guy's identity through his emails. They told me his name. I didn't know him. I had to file for an order of protection. The officer who served it called me afterwards to tell me how it went.

The cop said the guy insisted that he was my friend and said to the cop indignantly, "You're acting like I'm some kind of *stalker*."

Um, if the shoe fits….

I also had a cyber stalker who figured out how to "spoof" my Fox email address and send nasty emails to people, which appeared to be coming from me.

I had no idea this was happening until one day when I checked my email and found one from a colleague that said, "Yeah, well, I don't really care what you think."

What?

I scrolled down and saw an email with a header that said it came from my address, saying something very insulting to this guy. I was horrified!

I called the Fox Help Desk, and they were quickly able to determine that I had been "spoofed." They showed me the address the email had actually come from. It was a creepy fan who had been sending me three or four lengthy emails every day for months. It had started with a short email to which I gave a brief reply. Apparently, that was too much encouragement. He started emailing constantly. I never replied again, which angered him. He started escalating. But things had been quiet for a few days, so I had foolishly believed he had moved on.

Apparently not. He was getting revenge.

"But I don't understand," I told the tech guy. "When my colleague replied to the email, the reply came to *me*."

"Yes, that's how spoofing works. The reply comes to the real email address."

I emailed the colleague explaining what had happened, and he understood. But to this day, I wonder…was that the *only* email the spoofer sent? I was glad this colleague chose to respond, or I never would've known this was happening. But did other colleagues get weird emails from me and choose *not* to respond?

Although most people were friendly to me, I'll always wonder if any of my colleagues secretly distrusted me because of emails that I knew nothing about.

The police tracked down the cyber stalker in his state and told him to cease and desist. As with the others, he responded with denials and indignation. And this guy didn't go away. He stopped emailing and spoofing me (as far as I know), but instead started writing brutal comments about me on social media sites. Loyal fans forwarded me some of the comments he posted, just to make me aware. He was using his own name, but there was nothing I could do about his online vendetta. It all fell under the category of free speech.

I left my job in 2018. Mike and I had decided in June of 2017 that when my contract expired the following year, I would not renew this time. I informed Fox News in 2017, many months before my deal would be up for negotiation, that I planned to retire from the news. It was very amicable. I explained that I wasn't planning to work anywhere else in news. I would maybe do a little voice-over work, but I mainly wanted to spend more time with my husband and son. And I just didn't love my job anymore.

I had always known I wouldn't want to be in the news business forever. In fact, while I was still in my 20s, I was telling people I would leave the biz once I hit 50. I was over 50 when I quit, so I pretty much stuck to my life plan. I worked in broadcast news for 30 years. It was a good run. I made a living doing what I loved. But it was time to move on.

Working for a 24-hour news network has its pros and cons, but the older I got, the less I enjoyed the pros and the more I disliked the cons.

The bad hours were becoming more difficult to tolerate. Waking up early hadn't bothered me much when I was in my 20s. But by my late 40s, every time I did a morning show, when the alarm rang I thought to myself, "*I'm not getting up. They can fire me. I don't care.*"

I always managed to drag myself out of bed, but it was taking its toll. Eventually, I asked if I could switch to a part-time deal. Roger Ailes generously worked out a new contract under which I worked two or three days per week instead of five. I was very grateful that he granted my request. I had that part-time deal for four years.

The "catch" was that I had no specific shift. No longer anchoring the 5 AM show, my new job was to plug holes when anchors called in sick or took vacations. I happily agreed to this, since it was only two or three days a week. It was great at first. It enabled me to be home four or five days every week.

But it wore on me after a while. Sometimes I had plenty of notice regarding which hours I'd be working in a given week, but other times I was called at the last minute in the middle of the night because a morning anchor was out sick. I didn't have the option to say no, since my job was basically to sub for anchors as needed. So I was essentially "on call" 24/7. I never knew when I'd have to drop everything or get out of bed and go in.

The final straw for me was the day of a party for Colleen's two daughters. My goddaughter was graduating from high school, and her younger sister was turning "Sweet 16." Mike, Connor, and I drove to the state where they lived and were enjoying this big family party. Then I got the call: seven people had been killed in a terrorist attack in London. I had to come in to anchor four hours of live breaking news coverage overnight.

I sadly apologized to my nieces and the rest of my family. Mike drove me to the nearest railroad station, and I took the next train into Manhattan. During the hour-long ride, while reading up on this tragic story and contemplating the fact that I was going to be up all night covering it, I realized with certainty that I was "done."

By the time I got to work, my buzz from the two drinks I'd had at the party was long gone, but now I was crazy tired and my night was just beginning. I spent an hour in hair and makeup and four straight hours on the air in the middle of the night.

It was nobody's fault. The story had to be covered, and I knew what I was agreeing to when I signed up for this deal. But the lack of control over my life was too difficult.

I made it through the shift and got home early in the morning. After sleeping for hours, I told Mike it was time for me to retire. He wasn't surprised. I'd been talking about quitting for a while, and we had a financial plan in place to make it work. I even have a decent pension from Fox.

But the other times I'd contemplated retiring, Mike had tried to talk me out of it, saying I still seemed to enjoy my job, and he thought I would miss it. This time, he knew my decision was final, and he supported it.

The difficult hours were one issue, but there were others as well.

At that time, there was some drama regarding the sexual harassment scandal. I wasn't involved, but it changed the work atmosphere. Everyone was on edge.

And I suppose it's to be expected that after 17 years at the same job, there were a few people with whom I simply didn't get along. Although my overall experience at Fox was great, there were times when I was wronged. But this book is not about airing grievances. And dwelling on past slights is not healthy.

That said, I want to paint an accurate picture for those who are contemplating this career. It may look easy from the outside, but every job has its challenges.

As noted earlier, there are stalkers. One of mine was now impacting my whole family.

And news is depressing. We covered earthquakes, fires, murders, terrorism, disease, and political division. I was immersed in it all the time. After a while, it gives you the sense that the world is falling apart. It's difficult to set it aside when you're with family.

And there are many different pressures.

There's deadline pressure. A story has to be ready for the show, no matter how late it breaks. There's pressure to be first, even when the facts are still unclear. Fear of being scooped is a constant specter over a journalist's head.

There's pressure to be accurate, which often conflicts with the pressure to be first. A lot of bad information flies around when a story breaks. I named the source for everything I said, and I'm sure I overused the word "allegedly," but at times it was my only protection. Fortunately, I was never sued for anything I said on air.

There's ratings pressure. Our producers and executives pored over the numbers, checking how Fox News compared to its rivals in each time slot. They were especially interested in how we fared with adults between the ages of 25 and 54. That "key demographic" was the group advertisers most wanted to reach, so they were willing to pay more for spots in shows that did well in that demo. As I learned in my journalism classes, the TV business isn't about selling shows to viewers; it's about selling viewers to advertisers.

Another pressure I felt was trying to give viewers the full story despite time constraints. Guest segments were only three or four minutes long, so we didn't have time to fully "set up" each story with background information. We usually just gave a very broad summary of the topic before bringing in guests to opine on it. I sometimes tried to incorporate facts into my questions to fill that gap, but then my questions seemed long-winded, and guests had less time to answer.

Viewers sometimes criticize anchors for not "challenging" our guests enough when they make questionable points. But we rarely have enough time to go off on a tangent. If we do, the whole segment can go off course. And if we have two guests, they might talk over each other and then nothing productive comes out of it.

Anchors are also accused of giving more time to the "other side." It's difficult to moderate a segment in which both guests speak for the same exact amount of seconds. But I tried my best to be fair. A few times, if a viewer complained, I'd go back to the video and time out the entire segment, only to find that the difference in time given to each guest was literally 10 seconds or less. Yet viewers perceive things differently.

There are also growing demands for "ideological purity." Most people are not 100 percent conservative or liberal. Most deviate from the "party line" on at least one or two issues. But I would get attacked online by Fox viewers if I said something during a guest segment that came across as the least bit sympathetic to the "other side."

If I had just one guest and that guest was conservative, I considered it my job to play "devil's advocate." I'd try to articulate the liberal point of view as best I could, then give the conservative guest the opportunity to refute it. But some viewers were furious with me for even paying lip service to the other side. I considered that my job. Even if I personally agreed with the conservative, I was taught that journalists present both sides.

Another frustration was writer errors. Our writers were good, but they were under pressure and mistakes were made. I tried to look at every script in the computer before reading it on air, but some scripts weren't written until we were already live, so I had to read them cold. If those scripts contained errors, I was the one blamed by viewers.

Of course, anchors make our own mistakes, too. Especially when we have to go off script, we sometimes misspeak. Ad-libbing is difficult. And sometimes while we're talking, we're listening at the same time to a producer talking in our earpiece. Sometimes we lose track of what we're saying while focused on what we're hearing, and we end up blurting out something nonsensical.

Or we miss a guest's response entirely because the producer is talking in our ear. When a guest is remote, they're muted in our ear if a producer cuts in. So sometimes while a guest was talking, a producer would be in my ear giving me a lengthy rundown of what was coming up next. Then I'd ask the guest a question that he or she literally just answered without my hearing it, giving the appearance that I was daydreaming during my segment.

There is also the occasional technical mishap. If an earpiece stops working or prompter dies in the middle of a story, the anchor misses a cue or appears lost through no fault of their own. But viewers say the anchor was "caught napping."

And mistakes last forever. In this age of YouTube, a mistake isn't seen just by whoever happened to be watching it live. It's guaranteed to be posted online, where people who don't normally watch that anchor can gloat over their mistake for years to come.

Social media is unforgiving. I've had a few gaffes over the years, but no major errors. But after seeing how ruthless the critics can be of other anchors' mistakes, my fear of making a fatal error was becoming almost paralyzing.

Things have gotten even worse since I left. The cancel culture vultures are hungry to silence any voice with which they disagree.

There are left-wing sites whose sole purpose is to smear Fox News. On more than one occasion, I've seen items about myself on those sites containing totally false quotes. They literally have quotation marks around statements I never made. That's libel, and I could sue them for damaging my reputation, but who has the time for that? I just prayed every day that reasonable people would recognize that these sites are questionable and judge me instead on my actual on-air appearances, which they watched with their own eyes.

Knowing how tough it is out there, I greatly admire my former Fox colleagues who choose to remain in the line of fire. They take a lot of abuse in order to stand up for what they believe.

In addition to those with a political agenda, there are so-called "internet trolls" who insult people simply for their own amusement. It amazes me how cruel people can be to fellow human beings they don't even know. Total strangers would pick on my hair, clothes, jewelry, eyebrows, nails, even my crooked smile. And if I got 100 comments in a day and 99 of them were compliments but one was an insult, I would dwell on the one insult.

There are also miserable things called "click bait" articles. The writers post tantalizing headlines that function as "bait" to lure people to click on the article to read more. Once you click, the site's creator gets paid by advertisers whose ads are on the page you opened. There are several common click-bait articles that have been created for everyone who is even the slightest bit famous. One typically has the celebrity's name followed by "Affair, Boyfriend, Divorce."

Of course, when I saw the one with my name, I took the bait and clicked on it to see what was being said about me. The article said there was no indication that Patti Ann Browne is having an affair or has a boyfriend or is getting a divorce. Well, that was a relief but the damage was done. Once I clicked on that article, the advertisers got paid, and the article climbed up the search engine results for anyone who googled my name. The headline doesn't break any laws because it doesn't actually say I'm *having* an affair. It just spits out the words "Patti Ann Browne: Affair, Boyfriend, Divorce," and then the article itself says there's no hint of any of those.

Another popular click-bait headline promises to reveal the celeb's "net worth." How would anyone know that? And then there's the one called "Measurements." Among other things, the one for me claims to know my bra size. People actually believe this crap. Please folks, don't take the bait.

I had trained myself to shrug it all off, but my in-laws were really bothered by it. They worried that people would see the headlines and believe them. Mike's brother assured his dad, "Anyone with half a brain knows those sites are fake."

But my father-in-law responded, "Sadly, there are lots of people out there with less than half a brain." He's not wrong.

I found that my best strategy for staying sane was to stay off the internet. Unfortunately, that was no longer an option. Just as I was pulling away, Fox News was pushing its anchors to engage their fans on social media.

So now there was a new pressure added to all the others: pressure to get "follows." As with the other networks, Fox wanted us to post frequently to push up our views and likes. I enjoyed interacting with viewers online on my own terms, but I didn't like coming up with contrived posts for the sole purpose of garnering "likes." It was a world I wanted no part of, but in the 21st century, it could not be avoided. This was yet another reason I wanted to leave it all behind.

Another constant pressure in the television industry was the pressure to look good, especially as I got older. Since we were always chasing that younger demographic, it was clear that some executives favored younger anchors. I believe it's a misconception that younger viewers want their news from young anchors. When I was in my 20s, I knew I had a lot to learn. I didn't want the news from people my age. I wanted it from more seasoned professionals. I think that still holds true. Even when I was in my late 40s and early 50s, I got strong ratings in "the demo," suggesting that young people trust older anchors to give them the news.

Nonetheless I was feeling the pressure to look youthful. Unfortunately, beauty techniques that help anchors to temporarily look good actually ruin our beauty and health in the long run. Eyelash glue ruins your natural lashes. Mascara causes styes (especially if the same wand is used on multiple anchors). Heavy makeup clogs pores and deepens wrinkles. Over-styling damages hair follicles. Hair spray triggers asthma. Body shapers aggravate endometriosis and reflux. High heels wreck your ankles.

Many women in my business turn to more long-lasting solutions. Cosmetic procedures were popular among anchors at Fox and MSNBC. I did nothing for many years, but eventually I caved and had a few minor tweaks.

I have veneers on some of my upper teeth, as do many anchors.

Also, at a fairly young age, my chin started to sag, even when I was at my ideal weight. It made me look fat on camera. Viewers who met me in person would say, "You're so tiny! I thought you were a much *bi*gger girl."

So I got chin liposuction. It was quick and I was awake for it. It left a small scar under my chin, but my lower face is more defined.

My upper eyelids eventually started to droop, so I had a short procedure called a blepharoplasty, in which a surgeon cuts out some excess skin from the eyelid. Again, I was awake for it, and the recovery was pretty easy. And my eyes look much more open than they used to.

I also had a laser treatment on my face to burn off a layer of skin that my dermatologist said was full of pre-cancers. He recommended it after diagnosing me with my seventh or eighth skin cancer.

I was careless about the sun when I was younger, so I've had multiple basal cell carcinomas, as well as an early melanoma and a squamous cell carcinoma. One of the cancers was under my nose, and its removal left behind a small white round scar that doesn't cover well with makeup. Many times, people have told me that I have sweat or mayo above my lip. They mean well, but it's annoying.

Anyway, my doctor said I would be left with more surgical scars unless I removed the entire top layer of my face to catch the pre-cancers before they penetrated deeper. So the laser peel was for medical reasons, not cosmetic, but my dermatologist said it would "refresh" my face at the same time. I suppose it did, but I'm not sure.

I do not believe in Botox (it's made from the same toxin that causes botulism!) or fillers. I think they make some people's faces look weird. (But who knows, maybe other people are using them and I don't even know it because it looks natural on them.)

My face is showing signs of aging, and I have the condition known in pop culture as RBF ("Resting Bitch Face"), which basically means when my face is "at rest" I look like I want to kill someone. I'll be relaxing, perfectly content, and a friend will ask me what's wrong. Nothing's wrong, I'm just old and the corners of my mouth are pulling down. I think RBF should be renamed "ROF," as in "Resting OLD Face."

As a result, I'm tempted to do something about my jawline so I don't look angry all the time. But I don't want that "pulled" look, and I'm not on TV anymore, so I guess I'll just age gracefully from here on out.

I have never had any procedures whatsoever done on my body. I exercise and try to eat healthy. And sadly, my one pregnancy only lasted six months, which resulted in my avoiding stretch marks.

Due to all of the above pressures, I wasn't looking forward to going to the office anymore. I realize every job has its aggravations, and they don't all come with the rewards of being a news anchor. I knew I was lucky to be in my position. So, for decades I was willing to put up with the bad and focus on the good. But now I was just burned out.

Those were the "work factors." There were also issues on the home front. I had a sick dog to care for. Our beloved Hunter passed away a few months after my retirement, following a difficult decline. I wanted to be home with him full time at the end.

I also had a chronic ankle injury stemming from a fracture during a run years earlier, which needed to be addressed once and for all. I'd had surgery and was struggling to squeeze in rehab three days a week between work, helping Connor through home-work, and maintaining the household. There just didn't seem to be enough hours in the day.

And while Connor was doing great, I felt like I wasn't there for him enough. Even when I was physically there, I wasn't always emotionally "present." I was napping a lot, waking up groggy, ordering takeout instead of cooking, and just generally feeling too tired and irritable to give Connor and Mike my wholehearted attention. I was also having trouble staying on top of household chores.

"Work got my best, family got the rest," as they say. I was able to juggle better when I was younger. It was harder now. Something had to give.

Once I told Fox News I was leaving, I felt like a weight had been lifted off my shoulders. And I was able to look back on my career with no regrets.

Despite all the drawbacks I outlined above, I wouldn't trade a second of it. Journalism was my vocation. It was an exciting, energizing environment. I had a front-row seat to history. I reported on some of the most impactful events of our time. I got an adrenaline rush preparing stories for air, and I felt satisfaction seeing the final product.

There are thousands of women across the country who dream of a career as a TV news anchor. I got to live that dream. When I was younger, I wanted to be a teacher or a writer. I sort of became both of those as a journalist. I tried to explain and break down stories in ways that provided clarity, insight, and understanding.

I was inducted into St. Francis Prep's Hall of Fame and the Hall of Fame for the Diocese of Brooklyn (which includes Queens). I was able to bring my parents to some nice events where they got to rub elbows with "VIPs."

I emceed several sold-out galas for St. Francis Prep, as well as the sold-out "Night of a Million Lights" gala in Manhattan, which raised $625,000 for the autism charities Life's WORC and the Family Center for Autism. And every year since 2015 (except during the pandemic), I have emceed "Katie's Koncert," a fundraiser benefitting the Katie McBride Foundation in memory of Katie, who died at age 11 of a rare childhood cancer. That event always sells out.

Working in the TV business on a daily basis, I met movers and shakers: top-tier politicians; Olympic athletes; bestselling authors; astronauts; scientists; famous actors; comedians; rock stars; and other brilliant, caring people who made a difference in people's lives in a million different ways. Not all the news was bad. There were uplifting stories about "ordinary" people doing extraordinary things.

I also got to hear from many wonderful viewers through emails and social media posts. Although I mentioned the negative ones earlier, it was truly a pleasure reading most of the comments and an honor getting to know the viewers. I am still in touch with three guys from different parts of the country who call themselves "The PABketeers." Steve, Bob, and Tom have been with me through my struggles, and I have prayed for them through theirs. I am blessed with intelligent and caring fans, many of whom feel more like friends. I learned from them throughout my career, and their support buoyed me. And so many of them prayed for Connor during those dark days of the NICU. If you're one of them, I sincerely thank you for that.

I gave myself months to slowly empty out my office, filling a bag every day when I left. I wasn't around much during the last few months. I was only working two to three days per week anyway, and I was taking many of those days off to use up my remaining vacation days.

So it was a "soft exit." I said my goodbyes gradually as I bumped into people I might not see again. On my last day, I was given the opportunity to say goodbye on the air, but for some reason I didn't take it. I guess because most people thought I was already gone. And I didn't want viewers or the media to make a fuss over it and speculate about why I left. It really was "to spend more time with family" but nobody believes that line anymore. So I just said, "Take care, everyone!" as we went to black.

Before handing over my office keys and ID card, I wrote a brief but heartfelt email thanking my Fox colleagues for being my "second family" for more than 17 years.

I'm in touch with some of them in person and many more through Facebook, but I still miss them. Great group of people. Great place to work.

But to everything there is a season, as is written in Ecclesiastes. It was time for this long, gratifying season to end.

CHAPTER 14

Hunter

When I first spotted Hunter at a dog shelter on Long Island, it was love at first sight. It was the year 2000, and I was a single woman looking for a furry companion. The other potential owners walking through the kennel breezed past the cute little black and white dog curled up in the back of his cage. But I stopped and peeked in, and he looked me in the eyes and sprang up, tail wagging, and came right to the front as if to say "I've been waiting for you!"

I was instantly enamored with his sad brown eyes and big floppy ears. The woman said his name was Biscuit. I asked about his story. She had no information.

I asked to spend time with him in the area where people get acquainted with dogs they're considering adopting. He proudly clung to my side in the ring, gazing up at me adoringly, ignoring the other dogs and people. I'd been to several shelters and left without a pet. But I knew I wasn't leaving today without my new friend.

I was allowed to leave him in the ring to go to a separate room to sign the paperwork. When I came back, he was sitting upright at the edge of the ring, staring intently at the door through which I had disappeared. Instead of taking the opportunity to run around with the other dogs, people told me he sat there loyally the whole time, waiting for me to return. They laughed and said, "That dog chose you!"

It's true. He stole my heart.

I had always wanted a dog. My dad was allergic, so it was out of the question while I was young. Now I was living in Manhattan—a very dog-friendly city. People brought their dogs into bookstores and let them sit at their feet at sidewalk cafes, where waiters often provided water bowls and even treats. I sometimes worked long hours, but there were many excellent dog walkers in the city. My one-bedroom apartment wasn't huge, but my Upper West Side neighborhood had a few dog runs and was close to the parks.

I took "Biscuit" home and renamed him Hunter, since he reminded me of the hunting dogs with the horses in the classic paintings of English fox hunts.

His introduction to my apartment building didn't go great. I walked him to the elevator, and he wanted no part of that enclosed space. Terrified, he pulled away so hard he almost slipped his leash. There was no other way up, so I picked him up and brought him on with me. The doors closed and I put him down, and he promptly peed all over the elevator floor. I apologized to my neighbors, mopped up the mess, and wondered if I'd just made a huge mistake. I explained he was a brand new arrival and promised to train him, pronto.

House training him meant walking him every few hours at first, including the middle of the night. But he learned fast, and after a short time my neighbors seemed genuinely happy to see him in the halls. They would smile and say, "Hi, Hunter!" and bend down to give him a quick pat on the head. I was so grateful for their patience.

My apartment was a co-op and while dogs were allowed, a *disruptive* dog could get you thrown out of the building.

For the first few weeks, he howled loudly each day when I left for work. We're not talking about a quiet whimper. It was a prolonged, agonizing yelp like he was being tortured in my living room. I took him to obedience classes, where I was advised to distract him when I left for work each day by giving him chew knots and playing soothing music. I was also supposed to refrain from giving him a sad "goodbye."

These tactics worked to ease his separation anxiety. And he sure did love those rawhide treats. He liked to fling them in the air and then chase after them. I'd be home watching TV when a treat would fly past the screen, followed by Hunter darting it after it. It was more entertaining than *NCIS*.

I took Hunter to the vet, who told me he was still a puppy—probably five months old. This was a surprise, since the shelter told me he was full-grown. He was just 25 pounds, but the vet said he looked like a pure-bred German short-haired pointer who would grow to about 80 pounds. That was more dog than I had bargained for! I was relieved when Hunter stopped growing at around 33 pounds.

We took long daily walks in Central Park. You could go off leash in the Ramble back then, and he loved running around in the woods and climbing the rocks. He also joined me on some jogs in Riverside Park on the path along the Hudson River, but he had trouble holding back to my pace. He was very fast and liked to charge ahead to the end of his leash and then double back to me, panting, "Come on, keep up!"

On our daily visit to the dog run, he sped around like a bullet, daring the other dogs to race him. Many tried, but none ever beat him. You wouldn't know it to look at him, but he was crazy fast!

His instincts were a bit off, though. Once, he was minding his own business, sniffing around at the edge of the Central Park Lake, when a swan family spotted him from way across the water. The swan father angrily made a beeline for Hunter. If you've never seen a swan in attack mode, I must tell you it is terrifying! The swan puffed up his feathers into an enormous, menacing array, and started loudly beating his wings and hissing at Hunter. This guy had it in for Hunter, big time.

But Hunter just stared at the swan quizzically, tail wagging, head tilted, as if to say "Hello, Mr. Swan, how are you today?" I literally had to pull him away before the swan could attack. Aren't dogs supposed to have survival instincts?

Yet another time, we were in the park in the snow, and suddenly Hunter was pulling away. I looked down at him, and he was growling and bracing, staring at some threat off the path. I looked to see what it was, expecting to spot a mugger lurking in the bushes, and wishing I carried mace.

It was a snowman. Not a realistic looking snowman. Just three snowballs piled on top of each other with a carrot nose and button eyes. Hunter assumed a defensive stance and continued to growl, dodging left and right around the snowman, reacting as though the snowman were making sudden moves and had to be watched closely. Onlookers started pointing and laughing at my dopey mutt. I was mortified.

I asked him, "Really? The killer swan in full attack mode didn't scare you, but you're afraid of Frosty?"

Scary snowmen aside, Hunter loved the snow. No matter how old he got, when he played in snow, people mistook him for a puppy. He would bounce around in it like he was on a trampoline. Even if the snow was deep, he would blissfully plow ahead, turning to me with a snort, his face covered in white flakes, his wagging tail flinging snow left and right.

A couple of years after I adopted Hunter, I introduced him to my new boyfriend, Mike. Neither one was sure what to think. Mike was not a dog lover before Hunter. And Hunter was equally skeptical. As I recall, his exact words were: "Why is this other guy coming around? Things were great with just the two of us!" (I fancy myself a dog whisperer.)

So I read an article on how to get your dog to warm up to someone new. It said the "newcomer" should immediately give the dog a treat every time he showed up. The dog would quickly equate "Mike" with "Treat!" and be overjoyed by Mike's arrival. It worked. Dogs are simple creatures.

As for Mike, he soon admitted that as dogs go, Hunter was the best. Clearly Mike has good taste in companions. Even his parents, who were also not "dog people," came to love Hunter. They dubbed him their "Granddog" and gave him a present every Christmas.

I married him (Mike, not the dog), and a year later, our family grew to include Connor. He came home from the hospital with a noisy heart monitor and a baby's usual curiosity about a dog's fluffy tail and shiny eyes. Hunter was put off at first, but despite the chaos, he was gentle and protective of this new addition to our pack.

At the Christening party, baby Connor was asleep in his car seat in a corner of the room while we talked to guests nearby. At some point I glanced over and did a double take. There was Hunter, parked next to the baby, surveying the room, sitting like a sentinel keeping watch over his charge. Normally at a party Hunter would be scavenging for dropped appetizers or basking in the adoration of strangers. But he wasn't going to leave a member of his family unattended, even if it meant missing out on those delicious bacon-wrapped scallops!

Over the years, the magical love between boy and dog grew. I was always Hunter's number one, but once he accepted the fact that Connor was here to stay, he let him into his heart and came to appreciate the constant affection from the little boy whose name meant "hound lover."

Our whole family loved Hunter, even those who weren't dog fans. Relatives and friends who "dog sat" for him were always sad to see him go. Hunter especially liked his stays at Uncle Rob and Aunt Helen's "country house," full of long walks on the beach and lots of spoiling.

Hunter also enjoyed our visits to my parents' Hamptons house, especially romping around the marshes of their backyard pond and the nearby beach on Peconic Bay, where dogs were allowed off leash until a few years ago. But unlike many dogs, Hunter didn't like the water. It was nice to never have to worry about drying a smelly, wet dog, but we felt bad leaving him on the shore when we swam.

He also didn't like to stick his head out the car window—a unique pleasure for most dogs. If we rolled down a window in the back seat, he would cower on the other side. I thought maybe he'd feel safer with me. So with Mike driving, I'd sit Hunter on my lap and roll down the window and gently lean him toward it. He would wriggle away in a panic, seeming to think I was throwing him out the window.

"I'll stop shedding!" he would promise me with his eyes.

I gave up on that quickly. Maybe he had some leftover trauma from whatever led him to the shelter as a puppy. We did our best to make him feel safe and loved.

Walking Hunter was always an adventure. He didn't walk; he pranced. Whenever we took him out, he strutted proudly down the street with his absurdly long tail always way up and wagging furiously. No stranger could walk past him without commenting on how adorable he was. We met a lot of people that way. During our years of walking him in Manhattan, Mike and I met the entire cast of *Law and Order*. Even groups of "cool" high school boys would stop to gush over what a cute dog he was. Other dogs usually liked him, too, and paused to say hi (a.k.a. sniff butts). After moving to the suburbs, even the neighbors' cat, Marcel, eventually convinced Hunter to share his bed when Frank and Sharon watched him while we traveled.

Hunter wasn't so sure about other animals. Now and then we'd encounter a turtle in the yard of my parents' Hamptons house. Once, Connor picked one up, and Hunter, ever curious, came over and started gently sniffing it. The turtle quickly pulled its head inside the shell and wiggled its legs. Startled at realizing this object was alive, Hunter recoiled in fear and then started whimpering loudly, seemingly trying to warn Connor of the danger in his hand. Honestly, Hunter was more scared than the poor turtle.

We never knew for sure what breeds combined to make our perfect mutt. Speculating on breed mix is a popular pastime in Manhattan. Vets and random strangers all had opinions, but we never got him a DNA test, so we simply told people he was a "mystery mix."

He was too small to be a purebred German short-haired pointer, but he did seem to be at least part GSP. Part of the Sporting Group, pointers are considered friendly and willing to please. That described Hunter to a tee. He also did some "pointing" with his leg. At first, I thought he'd gone lame! I had a lot to learn about dogs. But he didn't point at squirrels or rabbits, as most pointers do. He had no interest in chasing small prey. Instead, he would bend his knee at the scent of the hot dog stand in the park. Some hunting dog.

Pointers supposedly have "strong retriever instincts." Hunter? Not so much. I'd throw a ball far away, and he'd eagerly chase after it, pick it up, turn to me proudly with the ball in his mouth, then drop it right there. He'd run back to me empty-handed and look up at me expectantly. "Do it again! Do it again!"

I'd say, "Dude, you forgot something." Still the eager look and the wagging tail, but no ball.

I'd say, "I need the ball," and I'd point to where he left it. Seeing my arm extend, he'd start sprinting away, head darting left and right, up and down, looking for the ball. Then he'd look back at me puzzled. "Where did it go? Didn't you just throw it? Did it vanish?"

Let's just say fetching was not in his skill set.

Pointers are also supposed to like catching balls and Frisbees in their mouths. The first time I tossed a tennis ball to Hunter to catch on the fly, it bonked him right on the nose. He looked at me stunned, like, "Why would you do that to me?" Pointers are described as smart. Maybe Hunter wasn't a pointer after all.

He was part beagle for sure. Hunter thankfully was not a barker, but when he chose to speak up, his baying made it instantly clear that he was a hound dog. When one of Colleen's daughters was very little, she was only familiar with two dogs: Hunter and Toto (Mary Lou and Jim's dog, who was pretty quiet). So at my niece's preschool, when asked, "What does a dog say?" she didn't go with the traditional "Woof!" Instead, she went with a deep-throated "Ah-WOOOOH!"

Hunter had a beagle's giant floppy ears and long tail. When Mike and I were about to sell our apartment, we were standing in our kitchen with a real estate agent, telling him how great the place was. Hunter, always looking for attention, was sitting nicely right in front of the fridge, looking up at the three of us with his most adorable expression. And then he wagged his three-foot-long tail (that's only a slight exaggeration). The tail swept under the refrigerator and out again, bringing with it the largest dust bunny I've ever seen. (He picked a great time to start bringing us rabbits.) I mean who sweeps under the fridge?

Some dog lovers insisted he was an English foxhound. He sure looked like the dogs in the paintings of "The Hunt." And it's possible there was some springer spaniel thrown in. But they're described as "bird dogs," and Hunter never showed any interest in birds.

And while he had a very keen sense of smell, its accuracy was questionable. I'd walk him along the curb of a Manhattan sidewalk, and there could literally be a discarded cheeseburger in the gutter, still hot. Hunter's nose would detect it from a great distance. His nostrils flaring, he'd pull hard toward that general area but then end up frantically sniffing a rock about a foot away. I would watch in amazement, wondering how long it would take him to figure out the rock wasn't edible and he had acquired the wrong target. Unfortunately for him, the answer was always: long enough that I had time to pull him back before he located the actual Big Mac.

Regardless of what breeds he was, the one trait Hunter had in spades was being lovable. If Connor or I started crying, he was there by our side, snuggling up against us, comforting us with his affection.

And when we were happy, he caught that contagion too. He would bound around with what I swear was an actual smile on his face, his tail wagging furiously. He was a full-fledged member of our family.

Hunter was so easy to love, when we asked my Uncle Rob and Aunt Helen to be his "guardians" should anything happen to us, they were so elated that I later joked to Mike, "How do we break it to them that we're not planning on dying any time soon?"

When we moved from the city to our house in the burbs, Hunter enjoyed the extra space. He had a yard to sniff around in, and he got lots of exercise following us from room to room—his favorite hobby. My mom called him "The Shadow."

Whenever we left, even just to put out the trash, Hunter looked longingly after us. We laughed hysterically at the movie, *The Secret Life of Pets*, when the woman leaves, and her dog immediately says sadly, "I miss her sooo much!" That was Hunter, for sure.

We never had to worry about Hunter wandering off. He liked to stay close. Once while I ran an errand, I got a call on my cell from our neighbor saying Hunter was sitting on our front lawn, and we didn't seem to be around. (A contractor was working on our kitchen and had left the side door open while going in and out for supplies.) Claire told me, "He's not going anywhere; he's just sitting there, but I thought you should know."

I told her I was around the corner, and when I drove up a few seconds later, I laughed. He was lying on the lawn on his haunches with his head up, lion-style, surveying the scene like the King of the Castle. When I got out of the car and he saw me, he didn't have a guilty look on his face. It was more like, "Oh hi, I held down the fort for you." (After that we locked him in a room whenever contractors came.)

Hunter wasn't allowed on most of our furniture, but there was a couch in the den that we let him claim. We put a covering on it so we could remove it for company. Well, that was an exercise in futility. Hunter was determined to rub his scent and hair into that couch. No matter what coverings we tried, he would paw at them until they came untucked and then roll around on the exposed couch. We'd vacuum and steam the couch once in a while. Again, a waste. It distressed him that his scent was gone, and his number one priority was putting it back.

Hunter had many nicknames through the years: Poochie-Pie, Puppy, Bubby, Bubblicious, Little Buddy, Dopey, Dumbo (the ears!). Sometimes we even called him Hunter.

Hunter was a loyal companion for 17 wonderful years.

In 2018, Hunter peacefully crossed over the Rainbow Bridge, at home with us hugging him, with a vet from the mobile pet hospice "Lap of Love."

We played gentle music and reminisced about all the happy times we'd had with our loyal hound. A photo slideshow of adorable Hunter photos played on our television. Father Sullivan from our parish said a prayer over him in his final hour. We read the "Creation Poem" and said the below prayers I found on the internet before and after his passing.

The vet snipped locks of his black-and-white hair for us, which we keep in a special box. And she pressed his paw into dye and then clay to make a colored paw imprint that sits on our mantle.

Not that we need it—as the saying goes, Hunter left "paw prints on our hearts."

CREATION POEM

When God had made the earth &
sky, the flowers and the trees,

He then made all the animals:
the fish, the birds and bees.

And when at last He'd finished,
no two were quite the same.

He said, "I'll walk this world of mine
and give each one a name."

And so He traveled far and wide,
and everywhere He went,

A little creature followed Him
until its strength was spent.

When all were named upon the
earth and in the sky and sea,

The little creature said, "Dear Lord,
there's no name left for me."

Lovingly God said to him, "I've
left you till the end.

I've turned my own name back to front
And called you DOG, My friend."

PRAYER OF FAREWELL

Loving God, Creator of all things
we know that not even a sparrow
falls without Your knowledge,
so we know that You are here with us today,
as our beloved pet Hunter makes his final journey.

Thank You for having entrusted us with such a loyal
and special dog.

Thank You for letting him teach us unselfish love.

Thank You for the memories of him that we can recall
to brighten our days for the rest of our lives.

Although we will miss Hunter dearly,
we thank You for allowing us to have so
many wonderful years with him.

Thank You for this and for all Thy blessings, Lord.

Finally, in gratitude, we return our pet Hunter to You
in Your Heavenly Kingdom. Amen.

Patti Ann Browne

PRAYER OF MOURNING

Almighty Father, We were blessed to
receive the gift of Hunter from You.

Now that he has left this life,
please help us cope with our loss
with strength and courage.

We know that our beloved companion
no longer suffers,
and will live on in many fond memories.

As he has enriched our lives,
we pray that we may enrich the
lives of others. Amen.

CHAPTER 15

Writing My Own Story

onnor is a teenager now and doing well. Once he hit middle school, he moved to a school that doesn't provide accommodations. I was nervous about their "sink or swim" approach, and I know it doesn't work for every child, but it has been highly effective for Connor.

Despite the dire predictions from NICU doctors of cognitive deficits, he is now on High Honor Roll at a selective Catholic high school, where he's on the Quiz Bowl team, and in the National Honor Society.

He's involved in lots of activities and has a group of friends with whom he texts way too often. In spite of supposedly "impaired lung function," he runs on the track team, plays tuba in the school band, and is in the hiking club.

A "chip off the old block," Connor anchors his school's morning announcements once a week, which are streamed live into every classroom and on the internet.

He moved up from Cub Scouts to Boy Scouts and is a member of the "Order of the Arrow" (the Scouts' National Honor Society). He's currently working hard on his Eagle Scout project and is on track to earn this highest honor in Scouting by the time this book is published.

He's in several religious clubs at his high school and is an altar server with our parish church.

We're so proud of the bright young man Connor has become. I hate to admit the "experts" had me worried that his early neurological deficits would hold him back in life. He still struggles, for sure. But he remains the fighter he was at birth, defying the odds and exceeding expectations.

For years, I bragged about his accomplishments in our annual Christmas card, because the folks who didn't see Connor regularly still remembered his rough start in life and wondered if he was doing okay. When I bumped into people I hadn't seen for years, they seemed almost afraid to ask how Connor was. So I felt compelled to assure everyone that he's doing great. But it's time to stop boasting, because I think I've convinced everyone by now.

But I also like to share Connor's progress to encourage the parents of other premature babies, and any kids with "issues." I urge you to disregard the "gloom and doom" speeches you might be hearing. I don't know why doctors and even some teachers focus on the worst-case scenario. Maybe the strategy is to prepare you for the worst, so that if things turn out better than expected, you'll be happy. But negative energy isn't productive. My advice is to stay positive. Your child will pick up on your optimism.

It's not always easy. It sometimes feels like a treadmill, with many late nights of homework devolving into shouting and tears. So we make a point of taking breaks from the daily grind to have fun. As a family, we've traveled with Mike's family to Hershey Park, Arizona, Disney, and Hawaii, where Mike was the best man in his brother Brian's wedding to my beautiful sister-in-law Suzanne.

With my side of the family, we've vacationed in Ireland, the Florida Keys, and the Hamptons. We've traveled to several states with Connor's track team. We go camping with friends from our neighborhood, and we love the beach, mini golf, and outdoor restaurants. Although it's sometimes difficult to squeeze in family time, that's the good stuff.

Once I quit my job, I was able to devote more time to helping Connor with the residual effects of his prematurity. He still had ADHD, OCD, and other issues, and I'd read that certain dietary strategies might help, as well as other lifestyle changes. But these all required time, which I didn't have while I was working. Now I can do more shopping and cooking, and stay on top of Connor's routine instead of collapsing on the couch.

I know I'm fortunate to be able to stay home. Many parents don't have that option, and some have more than one child, and some are single moms or dads. Yet they somehow make it work. I have so much respect for those parents.

I wish I could say, now that I have more sleep and less stress, that I'm the perfect wife and mom—always patient and with boundless energy for my family. But I'm not. I still get frustrated, and somehow the laundry still piles up. I have less energy than I used to, and I wonder if a small part of me misses the exhilarating work environment.

I certainly miss the hairdressers! I was so spoiled by having someone else do my hair all those years. These days it's rare for me to take out a blow dryer. I usually pull my hair back into a ponytail and get on with my day. I also frequently wear yoga pants, and my nails are not always painted. My life is less glamorous, but I have no regrets about leaving my job. I feel more engaged with Mike and Connor, and less zombie-like.

I'm definitely still busy. When I told my friends I was retiring, some warned me that I'd be bored. But actually, between projects, volunteering, and the usual demands of family, I always seem to have plenty to do.

For the first few months, I was caring for Hunter in his final days. He needed to be walked every two hours, given medications and special food, and carried up and down the stairs. He was also more anxious and attached to me, so I was glad I could be home for my old buddy during his sunset, instead of leaving him alone while I went to work.

In addition, I had my ankle injury to deal with. As mentioned, I had sprained and fractured my ankle during a run a few years earlier, and was in and out of a "boot" for a couple of years after that. Every time the boot came off and I re-started physical therapy, my Achilles tendon acted up, which is the drawback of immobilizing your calf for an extended period. I finally had surgery that left me in a cast, after which I had nerve damage and a bone spur. And my Achilles tendonitis was worse than ever. I was walking with a limp. So I was given an intensive physical therapy protocol that I would not have been able to follow had I stayed at Fox. I was at a rehab center three days a week for almost two hours, and had to follow a home regimen that involved stretches, exercises, icing, and compression throughout the day.

Eventually, I was able to walk long distances without pain, but I was told I will never run again. This was devastating news. I loved running. It relieved my stress and kept me fit, healthy, and happy. It also kept my asthma in check. I started swimming and cycling, but they're not the same.

So now I walk around my neighborhood. I still envy the runners who pass me, and I haven't completely dismissed the thought that I'll be able to run again someday. But I've come to accept that this is my new form of exercise for now, and I enjoy it. It's so important to keep moving, no matter what your fitness level. I'm a big believer in the benefits of exercise. Endorphins elevate my mood, and my brain functions more efficiently and creatively after a workout. Plus, sunlight curbs depression, provides Vitamin D, boosts immunity, and lowers the risk of certain cancers. So I'm glad I have the time to walk three miles every day.

After my ankle healed and Hunter passed away, a project came my way. One side of my family had an enormous reunion, after which we were all urged to work on our branches of the family tree before the next reunion three years later. Colleen started working on ours, but once her daughters were both away at college, she increased her work hours and activities.

So I offered to finish up the tree. What a monumental task! I was contacting family overseas, ordering documents like birth and death certificates, deciphering old handwritten letters, and emailing relatives to identify people in faded photographs. I discovered how important it is to talk with your oldest relatives about their family history—sooner rather than later. And label all your photos! It took months, but we now have a big fat binder full of pictures and anecdotes that bring our ancestors to life.

I also set up a home voice-over studio. Voice-over work was something I loved doing at Fox and prior jobs. Very often, if Fox needed someone to record some tracks for whatever purpose, they would ask me if I could pop down to the audio booth. It was always something that came easily for me and I enjoyed it.

So now I do the occasional voice-over project, although I must say it's a crowded field, and folks who do voice-overs for a living are aggressive about hustling for jobs. I do it more for fun and wait for jobs to fall into my lap. They do once in a while, but thankfully my family doesn't count on my voice-over income to eat.

Now that I'm not working, I have more time for recreational reading. I joined a book club soon after I retired, and I enjoy being able to dig into a fiction book or a memoir without feeling guilty about reading something other than news.

I'm also able to volunteer more. During my years as an anchor, I always felt guilty having to say no when an email went out asking for help with a charity event or other worthwhile cause in my neighborhood.

Now I can say yes. For more than three years now, I've been volunteering once a week with my church's food pantry, which serves as a reminder of how fortunate I am and how important it is to give back. I also enjoy chatting with my "pantry pals," Maureen, Tricia, and Noreen. We work hard but also have lots of laughs.

Through the food pantry, I also became friends with a neighbor whose daughter attends school with Connor. Mary stopped working with the pantry to take care of her adorable new grandson, but our friendship is one of the unexpected rewards that has come from volunteering in town.

I help out in other ways as well. When there are fundraising events in town, I can prepare raffle baskets and help out with a booth. I'm a lector at my church. I also still emcee events now and then, which is very rewarding.

When the pandemic hit, I dug my old sewing machine out of the attic and made masks. At first I donated them to doctors and nurses, since there was a shortage of masks for essential workers. Then after it became apparent that we were all going to be required to wear masks for a while, I started making them for friends and family and food pantry clients. I wanted them to have something comfortable and reusable so everyone wouldn't have to keep buying disposable masks.

I find sewing and some other home chores to be satisfying. I'm not exactly a domestic goddess, and I still hate laundry, but there is a certain appeal to being in a "support role" in my household, keeping things humming along behind the scenes.

The debate over women "Leaning In" vs. "Leaning Out" is still raging, years after it was started by Facebook COO Sheryl Sandberg. My high school classmate, Erin Callan, was the CFO of Lehman Brothers before its collapse. She contributed to the debate in 2013 with a much-discussed *New York Times* op-ed entitled, "Is There Life After Work?" That article resonated with me. She later turned it into a book, *Full Circle: A Memoir of Leaning In Too Far and the Journey Back.*

Every woman has to make the choice that's right for her. Some women thrive in a hard-charging career environment and have a lot to contribute to the workplace. That worked for me for a while too.

But once I had a family, I chose to "lean out," saying no to my bosses when their demands would interfere too much with my home life. I knew it might mean I'd be passed over for certain opportunities, and I was. But not everyone is willing to make the sacrifices required to climb all the way to the top. We really can't "have it all," but we can come close if we're willing to compromise.

We have to figure out what's important to us and write our own individual stories. *We* get to decide how far we want to go and how much we're willing to give up to get there.

There's no shame in leaning out or even walking away. Success isn't just about a job. For many people, it's about a happy, well-rounded life. Money is important, but wealth isn't necessary for happiness, and in some cases it can even be a detriment to it. I love my middle-class lifestyle. Mike and I both believe simple pleasures are life's greatest joys.

My husband also believes in giving back. A few years ago, Mike volunteered for a pediatric medical mission to Ecuador. He flew down with a team and spent a week assisting surgeons who operated on children with various health conditions that their local doctors couldn't handle. He's planning to go back in 2022.

Mike also volunteered to work some Covid shifts during the pandemic, after which he slept in our basement for weeks to avoid contaminating Connor and me. It was a sacrifice, but he wanted to pitch in. None of us got the virus.

Mike serves on our church's Parish Council and is a member of the Knights of Columbus, along with his dad, my dad, and my brother-in-law. The "K of C" is a Catholic fraternal organization with two million members worldwide who do community service. Mike's chapter runs an annual blood drive, which is often the largest by an organization on Long Island. The chapter also conducts fundraisers benefitting various charities including a fantastic program called "Rock Steady Boxing," which helps Parkinson's patients improve their balance, motor skills, and gait.

Nationally, the Knights are on the scene of many natural disasters. And as Kathryn Jean Lopez notes in *National Review*, they successfully petitioned the Obama administration to recognize the Islamic State genocide in Iraq. They've been advocates for racial justice for more than a century. They had black members as far back as the late 1800s and defended black people against the KKK in the 1920s. They provide support for immigrants and refugees. I'm glad Mike is part of this organization and has the chance to bond with other Catholic men doing charitable works.

Mike is a good guy. And I'm sorry to disappoint the online gossips, but despite the inevitable ups and downs, we are still happily married. After 18 years together, we've only had three fights—the same three fights, over and over again.

I thought about that joke recently, and realized I could say the same thing about sins: "In my entire life, I've only committed three sins—the same three sins, over and over again." Okay, it's probably more than three, but the point is I'm no saint. I have my faults, and they're mainly the same ones I've always had, despite trying to work on them. I have regrets, and I can only wake up each day and strive to do better.

My faith helps me to be a better person. I know not everyone is religious, and the church's story has had dark chapters—in its distant past as well as its recent history, and even its present. I completely understand how these scandals have driven people away from their faith. I hope Catholic leaders will resolve, once and for all, to put a stop to the shameful behaviors that have left stains on the church and tainted the wonderful work of truly devout Catholics. These scandals are a reminder that humans are flawed, and evil is all around us.

But the Catholic Church has been a force for good in many ways. The organization Catholic Charities provides food and affordable housing for the poor, services for immigrants and refugees, safe houses for battered women, HIV treatment, and counseling for women who regret abortions, among many other things. And while Pope Francis is far to my left politically, I am happy to see his statements encouraging Catholics to welcome and love homosexuals.

For me personally, the church has always been a source of strength and comfort. I've been blessed to be influenced by church leaders who have maintained their integrity while some around them have been corrupted. They promote tolerance and acceptance. They preach forgiveness and understanding. They are examples of God's most important commandment: love one another.

I'm fortunate to be part of a strong local parish full of both young families and prayerful older folks who attend Mass regularly and are active in the church. Our leadership encourages a "culture of caring," urging us to reach out to those in need, treat others with kindness, and reject pettiness and hypocrisy.

Being involved in my parish has motivated me to look at myself honestly, avoid complacency, and recognize the areas in which I could do better. I'm a pretty good person, but I've also been blessed with many gifts. In the Bible, Luke says, "From everyone who has been given much, much will be demanded."

Have I done everything I can? I'd like to do more. In the Parable of the Talents, Jesus makes a similar point and warns: "Be on the alert, for you do not know which day your Lord is coming."

Since retiring, I've had some somber reminders that life is short. Colleen's husband, Mike, had a major health scare years ago. A previously undiagnosed malformation of the blood vessels in his brain triggered a life-threatening brain hemorrhage that caused a series of seizures and led to risky brain surgery a few months later. Thank

God, he got through it successfully and is now healthy and fit and stronger than ever.

When he left the hospital back in 2013, Mike asked the neurologist what he could do to make sure this never happens again. Her instruction was simply: "*Live life with a leap of faith.*" Colleen put that advice on a plaque hanging in their house. They've been happily following it ever since. Words to live by for us all.

In 2019, my friend Lajja passed away after a long battle with breast cancer.

I went to high school with her husband, Ron. Decades later, Mike and I had just purchased our house when I bumped into Ron at a party with other St. Francis Prep alumni. He asked where we were moving. I named the town. He and Lajja literally lived around the corner. Ron asked if he could offer any help or advice about moving into our new neighborhood. I mentioned needing to find services for my three-year-old son, who had been born premature.

"You're asking the right person," he said. "My son Aidan is the same age. He was also born premature, and my wife Lajja knows everything there is to know about resources for special needs kids."

It was one of those serendipitous encounters. Ron introduced me to Lajja, and she went out of her way to welcome us to our new village, and shared with me her wealth of knowledge about therapists and programs. Lajja was a dynamo. She had so much on her plate, but she never seemed tired. She just kept going, fighting for her son and still finding the time to help others like me.

We started going out to dinners every few months with Ron and Lajja and a few other couples from our class year at Prep. We had so many laughs together for 10 happy years.

Mike, Connor, and I were on vacation in Florida when Lajja passed away. We had said our goodbyes before leaving, but I hated not being there for the services.

Connor and Aidan are still friends, and Mike and I are still close with Ron. As of this writing, Ron has found happiness with a terrific woman from our high school. It's too soon to know where it's headed, but we're glad Ron has found a companion to help him through these tough times. His house is still adorned with beautiful photos of Lajja. She will never be forgotten.

Tragically, in 2020, there were many more reminders of life's fragility. The coronavirus hit New York hard. My Facebook feed was like an obituary page. Many of my friends lost their parents, and others lost siblings and spouses who were my age, despite the widespread misconception that only the elderly were dying.

Several of my friends were hospitalized and recovered, and reported that it was the worst thing they had ever experienced. The majority of my friends who got Covid-19 experienced only mild symptoms, but a few barely survived.

My old gang from the McDonald's where I worked as a teen has a private Facebook group. In March of 2020, my former co-worker, Joe, posted that our 57-year-old friend, Rich Beseler, was hospitalized on oxygen with the coronavirus and needed our prayers. This chilling post from Joe came the following day:

> *Last night Rich was intubated and had to be placed on a ventilator to assist his breathing. Doctors are treating him with anti-malarial, antivirals, antibiotics, and HIV meds in a multi-pronged effort to battle this infection...I am worried for my friend and can't imagine being in a world with-*

out him. That being said, I know he is strong and will pull through. I'm doubling up on my prayers immediately!

For two weeks, things looked very grim. Rich remained on the ventilator, running a fever on and off. His liver and kidney functions were starting to decline, and he was unconscious the whole time. We all prayed fervently, and on Easter Sunday we got this post from Joe:

Well, it seems like the man upstairs has decided to answer all those prayers on the holiest Christian day of the year. Rich is awake and alert and is able to follow nurses' movements with his eyes. Doctors have stopped many of his meds and the prognosis is that they expect him to be on the road to a full recovery.

It was an Easter miracle! A few days later, after 16 brutal days on the ventilator, Rich was taken off the machine. But getting off the ventilator was just the first step in a long journey toward recovery.

He still had a trachea tube in place for a while and could not speak. It took him weeks just to sit up in a chair in the hospital, and months before he could stand and walk with a giant walker and two aides. Transferred to a rehab center, he was finally able to eat on his own three months after being taken off the vent. It was more months until he could use his left hand.

I saw Rich and Jeanne almost a year after his hospitalization. He looked great! He was still working to regain full use of his right hand, and the ventilator damaged his vocal cords, but he was happy to be alive and taking long walks on the Jones Beach boardwalk.

Rich and I are both vaccinated. But despite all he went through, Rich shares my concern that some measures to curb this virus have their own serious consequences. He also wishes it all hadn't become so politicized. But Rich's biggest takeaway is to cherish life. He says he's grateful for everyone's prayers, and the experience has renewed his faith.

One day, when I was teaching Faith Formation (after-school Catholic education for public school students), a student asked why we should believe in something we can't see.

I said God is so much bigger and smarter than we are that it's impossible for us to comprehend. I described a scenario in which a fly gets stuck inside your house, and sees the light from a window so it keeps banging against the window pane.

"You open the window so the bug can fly out and be free. But the fly can't see the open window below the individual pane it's on. The fly is too small to see beyond the frame surrounding it.

"But you, being a human, are so many times bigger and smarter than that fly. You can see the big picture that the fly can't comprehend. The fly needs guidance from a force beyond itself.

"So you gently nudge the fly toward the opening. But the fly stubbornly thinks it knows the best way out. Its brain is so small, it can't understand that the giant human is smarter and can see things it can't see.

"If only the fly would trust the human to guide it. If only we would trust God, who sees all, when He tries to nudge us in the right direction."

At this point one of my third graders raised his hand, rolled his eyes, and asked, "Why not just kill the fly? That's what *we* do when a fly gets into *our* house!"

Hmmm. He might've missed my point. Perhaps being a teacher wasn't my calling after all.

Anyway, trust in a higher power is the underlying theme of this book. I didn't necessarily understand that when I started writing. But as I reflected on my experiences and put it all into words, I realized how many times God was there for me—times when sudden twists of fate worked out for me, or people said things at just the right time. God speaks to us in strange ways and through surprising people.

There were times when I refused to listen. I sometimes pushed God away. There was even a period when I stopped going to church. Looking back now, it's clear to me that those were some of my darkest, most confusing times. If I tried to manipulate situations to control things outside my control, I was not my best self and my efforts backfired. It wasn't that God abandoned me. As the talented artist Sia suggests in her song, "Footprints in the Sand," we sometimes neglect God, and disregard the voice in our head trying to guide us to better decisions.

And prayer only works when it's backed up by positive actions, not cynical behavior.

I truly believe the adage that God helps those who help themselves. I've become aware of divine intervention—unexpected rewards that seem to come when I make better choices and trust that things will work themselves out.

When I sat down to write this book, my intention wasn't to get it published. Other people have had much more exciting lives. I was just following my mom's advice to write down all my life's adventures before I forget them. But when I showed some chapters to friends and family, they encouraged me to try for a book deal. This would've made more sense while I was still at Fox, except that I was far too busy to write a book while I was working. But once I left, I was writing it anyway, so I sent out my book proposal, with the understanding that it might not lead anywhere.

I was surprised and flattered that my humble story generated interest among several publishers. Once I had a book deal and realized my story would be "out there" in the world, the writing process became more daunting. But as Harris Faulkner notes in her excellent memoir, 9 *Rules of Engagement*, "if you can just reach up and easily grab something, it probably doesn't have a lot of value. Your effort has to match your purpose."

She also points out that we need to keep reaching for new goals in order to grow and move forward in life. This book was a growing process for me. And now I dare to hope that some of my little anecdotes might just uplift other people. That is my sincere wish.

In June of 2021, when pandemic restrictions began to ease, Mike, Connor, and I were finally able to gather with my entire extended family once again, at a party for my goddaughter's college graduation. This time, I was able to stay until the end! My parents were there, along with my sisters and brothers-in-law and their kids and significant others, including Patrick and Stephanie. We took a new family portrait. Looking around at my loved ones, I was filled with gratitude. Every one of them is a blessing in my life.

My story isn't finished. God willing, I have many more chapters to write. And so far, all signs point to a Happy Ending.

ACKNOWLEDGMENTS

To my favorite dance partner, Mike…I'm so lucky to be dancing through life with you. Thank you for holding me up through all our dips and spins. I could never have written this book without your support and inspiration.

To my precious son, Connor…I feel so blessed to be your mom. While I try to teach you the lessons you'll need for life, you have taught me more than I could ever imagine. I am so proud of the young man you have become. I love you always.

To my parents…thank you encouraging me to finally write a book and for your unwavering belief in me. You are the wind beneath my wings.

To Colleen and Patrick…thank you for allowing me to tell your beautiful story. I believe it will inspire others.

To my early readers, Mary Lou, Delanie, and Molly…thank you for reviewing my rough manuscript and giving me honest yet kind-hearted advice on how to make it better.

To the rest of my extended family…thank you for reminding me of stories I'd forgotten and for being a special part of my life. I love you all!

To Janice Dean…your support and encouragement meant so much!

To my publisher, Anthony Ziccardi, and the rest of the Post Hill team including managing editor Maddie Sturgeon, Cody

Corcoran, Devon Brown, and Holly Layman...thank you for putting my words into print and for your steadfast belief that many different voices should be heard. (And for letting me use AP-style numbers.)

To photographer Barry Morgenstein...thank you for somehow always making me look 10 years younger and 10 pounds lighter.

To attorney Michael O'Connor with Williams & Connolly... thank you for helping to make my dream of signing a book deal a reality.

To Fox News...thank you for 17 good years and for helping me share the news of my book.